PRAISE FOR DEBRA LAWLESS'S *CHATHAM IN THE JAZZ AGE*

"Everyone knows that Chatham enjoys some of the most spectacular scenery of any East Coast resort. What we may not know is that great resorts are not just discovered, they are made. In this charming book Debra Lawless chronicles how Joseph Lincoln, Alice Stallknecht and others used their talents to create and sell the idea of Chatham and Olde Cape Cod to the world as it dashed madly into the fun and frivolity of the new Jazz Age."

—William Sargent, author of numerous books on Cape Cod's coastal environment, including *Just Seconds from the Ocean: Coastal Living in the Wake of Katrina*, 2008

"I have just finished *Chatham in the Jazz Age*. I liked this book a great deal. As a native Chatham man with Eldridge/Nickerson bloodlines, I know a bit about Chatham and its history. Debra's neat little book opened my eyes to facets of Chatham that I knew little about. She writes well and in a manner that makes the reader want more. Great pictures as well."

—Dana Eldridge, a thirteenth-generation Cape Codder and the author of three memoirs, including *A Cape Cod Kinship*, 2008

from

THE SECOND WORLD WAR
TO THE AGE OF AQUARIUS

debra lawless

Charleston London

THE
History
PRESS

Published by The History Press
Charleston, SC 29403
www.historypress.net

Front cover: photo by Leroy Aaronson.
Back cover: original watercolor by Kathrine Lovell.

First published 2010

Manufactured in the United States

ISBN 978.1.59629.886.6

Library of Congress Cataloging-in-Publication Data

Lawless, Debra.
Chatham : from the Second World War to the age of Aquarius / Debra Lawless.
p. cm.
Includes bibliographical references.
ISBN 978-1-59629-886-6
1. Chatham (Mass.)--History--20th century. 2. Chatham (Mass.)--Social life and
customs--20th century. I. Title.
F74.C43L38 2010
974.4'92--dc22
2010008784

Notice: The information in this book is true and complete to the best of our knowledge.
It is offered without guarantee on the part of the author or The History Press. The
author and The History Press disclaim all liability in connection with the
use of this book.

For Stuart Stearns
Friend, mentor

Contents

Acknowledgements

I owe a great debt to the many generous people who have helped me try to answer the question: What was life in Chatham, Massachusetts, like between 1939 and 1969?

I thank: Gene Guild for sharing family recollections and photographs; Robert Hardy for detailed background information; Roslyn Coleman for her tour of Ship's Light, Dr. Minnie Buck's former house; Alia Zara Aurami for her recollections of Alice Guild and her grandmother Minnie Buck; Reggie Nickerson for his memories of Minnie Buck and Alice Stallknecht; Henry Schalizki for his vivid wartime descriptions of Chatham; Stuart Stearns for his dedicated research into the technology of World War II and radar; Richard Kraycir for information about Station C Chatham; Harry Cutts for his memories of bombings over Monomoy; Ginny Nickerson for her photo of her father and many insights; Jan Woolf Bilhuber and Bill and Nancy Husted Koerner for their detailed recollections of summers working at Hawes House; Lonnie Pickett for photographs and insight into Chatham's radar; Fred Byrne for his recollections of the 1960s; Don and Hannah St. Pierre for their memories of the 1960s; Rick Smith for sharing family photographs and anecdotes about Woodstock 1969; Jack and Bess Moye for reminiscing about their lives in Chatham and the development of Riverbay; Judith Llewellyn and Marilyn Brown for their encyclopedic memories of Chatham; Elizabeth Freedman Doherty for her dogged research into the archives of MIT's Lincoln Laboratory; archivists at Mitre Corporate Archives; Mary Ann Gray for her ideas and archival aid; Amy Andreasson for her reference help; Eric Linder for many amusing literary conversations and for alerting me to Sylvia Plath's visits to Chatham; Kassie Foss for her original pen-and-ink artwork and friendship; William Camiré for his photograph of Monomoy; Caitlin and Joanne Doggart for fun book signings; author Stephanie Schorow for her early encouragement; and friends at the Chatham Historical Society, the Eldredge Public Library and The History Press. I have in many instances relied on reporting I did for the *Cape Cod Chronicle*, and I thank my many friends there.

On a personal level, I thank my dear friends Kathrine Lovell, a talented artist; Susan Huling; the Deane Folsom families; Sally Wightman; Mary Siqueiros; and the daughters of the late Jack Collins—Margaret Burns and Kathleen Collins. Jack's friendship was a gift that lasted until his death in January 2010. I thank Emma Willard's class of 1977—pals for life. I thank my father, Leroy Aaronson, and most of all, I thank my wonderful husband, John.

Introduction

Chatham is 'Our Town,'" a friend said. He had just read *Chatham in the Jazz Age*, my book about Chatham from the early part of the twentieth century to the eve of World War II. *Our Town* is, of course, Thornton Wilder's famous 1938 play set in the fictional town of Grover's Corners, New Hampshire.

Our Town begins in May 1901. At that time, Chatham, like Grover's Corners, was defined by a Main Street, a railroad station, a post office, a school and a town hall. Social life revolved around churches of various denominations (three in Chatham,[1] five in Grover's Corners). In both towns, the earliest tombstones date to the late seventeenth century, and both towns were run by a board of selectmen, were mainly Protestant and Republican and had only a "sprinkling" of professional men. Compared to Chatham's 1910 population of 1,564, Grover's Corners, with its population of 2,642, was teeming.

The play centers on the families of two of the professional men—Doc Gibbs and Editor Webb, who publishes the twice-weekly newspaper. While telling the story of these families, the play poses larger questions about life's profound moments: birth, courtship, marriage, motherhood, death and grief.

Chatham painter Alice Stallknecht captures something of this same world in her cycle of three murals, beginning with *Christ Preaching to the Multitude* in 1931, continuing with *The Circle Supper* in 1935 and ending with *Every Man to His Trade*, completed in 1945. In *Every Man*, we see the life cycle from birth, in an upper left panel, to death, in the lower right. The town's Methodist and Congregational churches flank the tableau. Stallknecht depicts the town's

Alice Stallknecht depicted the
selectmen giving money to a
needy resident in her 1945
mural *Every Man to His Trade*.
The three selectmen also bore
the moniker "overseers of
the poor." *Photo by the author
from a painting at the Chatham,
Massachusetts Historical Society.*

fishing heritage and nods to the all-important tourism industry by depicting
a couple standing in front of the Hawes House sign. We see a farmer, a town
meeting and ladies running a shop.

Perhaps the greatest difference between Grover's Corners and Chatham
is that the residents of Grover's Corners did not engage in a marketing
campaign to lure visitors to their town. They seemed content on their own.

Viewing Chatham through the lens of *Our Town* isn't as fanciful as it
might seem. Thornton Wilder spent a part of three summers in the 1920s
in Chatham with the Townson family at their house, Sur Mer.[2] He had been
tutoring Douglas Townson's much younger brother Andrew, nicknamed
Mutt, a prep school student with "sort of a behavior problem," and during
the fall of 1926, Wilder and Mutt toured Europe. During his visits to the
family home in Chatham, Wilder outlined *The Bridge of San Luis Rey* in the
windmill on the property.[3] The Townsons' Shore Road house was next
door to Joseph Lincoln's house, Crosstrees, and one wonders if the path
of Lincoln, also a novelist and playwright, ever crossed that of the young
Wilder, who would win three Pulitzer prizes.

While Chatham had, in the years after its 1912 bicentennial, re-created
itself as an established tourist town with a two-month "season," Pearl Harbor

Day and World War II temporarily halted this enterprise. In the early part of the century, Chatham's story revolved around the townspeople's conscious efforts to lure visitors. During the middle part of the century, Chatham was a victim, if you will, of its own coastal geography. Three branches of the military—the U.S. Navy, the Army Air Forces and the Coast Guard—all found Chatham's coastal position thirty-five miles out to sea to be strategic.

After the war, as soldiers returned and the baby boom began, life resumed in a different form; it seemed that young families were everywhere. Chatham also lured retirees. Vacant stretches of land were cleared of pitch pines and carved into subdivisions in the 1950s. At the same time, tourism kicked into high gear with a drive made easy along the new Mid-Cape Highway to exit 11. Motels cropped up on Route 28. The summer rental industry boomed. By the 1960s, tourists were no longer looking for "quaint Cape Cod" and the "old salt." They wanted sun, sand and fried seafood—somewhere to take the kids on a rainy afternoon. It seems that, from the 1940s on, as the world shrank, Chatham was less able to control its own destiny and became but a player on the stage.

In this book, I will try to delve into the psyche of this one small town—its secrets, dreams and aspirations as it matured, decade by decade—and in so doing I hope I may hit upon a universal truth about life as it was lived in the now-vanished world of the middle part of the twentieth century.

Wartime at Home

He was a famous trumpet man from old Chicago way
He had a boogie style that no one else could play
He was the top man at his craft
But then his number came up and he was gone with the draft
He's in the army now, a-blowin' reveille
He's the boogie-woogie bugle boy of Company B.
—*Don Raye and Hughie Prince, 1941*

THE DEATH OF ROBERT SCOTT BROWN

Robert Scott Brown, known to his friends and family as Scotty, had a peculiar habit. On cold winter mornings, he often walked from his home on Seaview Street to Chatham High School with wet hair. By the time he reached the Main Street school, his brown hair was white. It had frozen.

Like everyone who knew Scotty, Bob Hardy, who was two years behind Scotty in school, describes him as a "great guy."[4] Scotty and Bob's older brother Jim, both members of the class of 1935, "used to chum around."

Scotty had spent his childhood in Concord; when he was in his early teens, he and his widowed mother, Mrs. Lena Ayers, had moved to a house on Seaview Street that backed up onto a golf course. In school, Scotty went in for wrestling. "He was kind of a muscleman," Hardy recalls. In fact, at Chatham High School, Scotty was an outstanding athlete. An undated photograph of Scotty shows a man with a broad grin. His blue eyes nearly match the blue of his necktie.

Private Robert Scott Brown at Hickam Field, Pearl Harbor. Brown sent this photograph to his mother, Lena Ayers, who lived on Seaview Street. Brown, a 1935 graduate of Chatham High, was the only Cape Codder killed at Pearl Harbor on December 7, 1941. *Photo courtesy of the Chatham, Massachusetts Historical Society.*

After graduating, Scotty enlisted in the Army Air Forces, as it was then called. After basic training, the military offered Scotty a choice of stations. Perhaps thinking he would see something of the world—or perhaps craving a warmer climate than Chatham—he chose Hawaii, where he was a private in the Eleventh Bombardment Group. Scotty was now a long way from his home on Seaview Street, a fact made poignant when he spotted a sign at Hickam Field in Oahu that pointed east to Boston, 6,328 miles away. ("Whew!" he wrote.)

One evening, Scotty, then twenty-six, flew in the Plexiglas nose of a B-18 Bolo bomber plane.

"It seemed like we were floating through space, which we were at five thousand feet," Scotty wrote to Mrs. Ayers in September 1941. "There was a half-moon and it shone on the Pacific as we headed for Port Allen on the Island of Kauai."

It is hard to imagine what impression Mrs. Ayers, who most likely had not flown in an airplane, had of her son's nighttime flight over Hawaii. "As we returned the lights on Honolulu were beautiful and the search-lights from the different parts of the Island [were] trying to pick us up."[5]

As he continued though training courses at Hickam, Scotty often wrote to his mother and sent her photographs of himself under palm trees. He filled his mother in on his news, such as his grades in various courses leading to his diplomas in aircraft armorers, chemical warfare and ground defense. And speaking of his older friend in Chatham, Wendell Rogers the painter, Scotty wrote, "Wendell said he would like to paint a picture of four old men sitting around a table in easy chairs in the middle of Main Street, playing poker. He said he'd call it 'Chatham after Labor Day.'"

The joke was, of course, that Chatham cleared out so completely after Labor Day that, as people often said, you could shoot a gun down Main Street without hitting anyone.

Shortly before Scotty left home for his military training, he ran into a young woman named Charlotte Forgeron in the post office.[6] He promised Charlotte, who was going to be a teacher, that he'd send her a little alligator from Florida. Now Scotty wanted his mother to send him items from home: a suit and a pound of tobacco. In a later letter, Scotty acknowledged receipt

Wendell Rogers painted this snowy view of Main Street in about 1940. At right are the old movie theatre and Universalist church; at left is Rogers's art studio. Rogers's easel would have been in front of the Congregational church. *Photo courtesy of the Chatham, Massachusetts Historical Society.*

of his suit, watchband and tobacco. He asked Mrs. Ayers to send another pound of tobacco. He told her that the sultry actress Dorothy Lamour was at the field autographing photos. And he told her of a lighthearted moment at the squadron beer party when the enlisted men threw Captain Rasmusen, the new squadron commander, into the water. "They really let the bars down on these occasions," he said.

On Thanksgiving Day 1941, Scotty and the other soldiers at Hickam Field dined on turkey, ham and pumpkin, cherry and mince pies and finished their meals with fresh lemonade, coffee, fruits, nuts and bonbons. They smoked a few cigars and cigarettes as they digested their feasts.

Back home in Chatham, December began with unseasonably warm weather. In some places, pussy willows were budding.

On Sunday, December 7, Lena Ayers, alone in her house on Seaview Street, was listening to the radio after lunch when she heard that the Japanese had bombed Pearl Harbor. She was terrified, thinking of her son.

"The United States, which no foreign power would ever have the effrontery to attack, had been attacked," Chatham's novelist Joseph C. Lincoln wrote in his wartime novel, *The Bradshaws of Harniss*.[7]

> *Zenas Bradshaw's first sensations were, like those of all his fellow Americans, amazement, shock, and then a furious desire to fight. He sat up far into the night listening for the last scrap of news the radio could give him and went to bed to toss and tumble.*

On Monday, December 8, Congress declared war on the Japanese Empire. Chatham High senior Phil Nickerson and about eight of his classmates left the Main Street school in the middle of the day to hear Roosevelt's speech to Congress on a radio owned by Ben Rollins, Chatham's motorcycle cop. Upon returning to school, the classmates were surprised that they did not get into trouble.[8]

Time must have stretched unbearably as Mrs. Ayers waited. On Tuesday, still with no word, Mrs. Ayers decided to travel to her sister's house in Newton, where at least she would not have to wait alone. Travel that day was not easy as the Cape and eastern Massachusetts were on the alert for enemy airplanes after a "strange aircraft" was seen off the East Coast.[9] "Heavy United States Army or Navy patrol bombers passed over Cape Cod at dawn today and twice this morning," the *Cape Cod Standard-Times* reported.

In Chatham, Sabin "Slim" Hutchings, who had repeatedly posed as Christ for muralist Alice Stallknecht, headed the public safety committee, which organized a state guard reserve unit. Nine air raid wardens, under the direction of George Goodspeed and Parker Romkey, were covering seven areas of Chatham that had been designated as air raid listening posts. The following day, they announced that nine blasts of the fire siren, repeated continuously for five minutes, would warn residents of an approaching air raid. The "all clear" would be eighteen blasts. Still no word had come to Chatham about Scotty Brown; Louis Thacher, in the Army Medical Corps in Hawaii; or Robert Matheson, on the USS *Chester* in Pearl Harbor.

It was probably Thursday when Mrs. Ayers's neighbors on Seaview Street directed a man trying to deliver a telegram to Mrs. Ayers's sister's house in Newton. Telegrams so often meant bad news. One can imagine Mrs. Ayers's trepidation as she opened the telegram that had followed her.

Mrs. Ayers now knew: her son Scotty was dead.

As the first wave of bombings began on that morning of December 7 at Hickam Field, Scotty, "conspicuous for his bravery," assisted in repairing an airplane. "Later a severe attack of bombing and strafing was centered on the

The painter Wendell M. Rogers (1890–1973) was a good friend of Scotty Brown, the only Cape Codder killed at Pearl Harbor. Rogers, who created over three thousand works, often painted en plein air, sometimes clad in his woolen bathing suit. *Photo courtesy of the Chatham, Massachusetts Historical Society.*

hangars," a later document accompanying Scotty's posthumous Silver Star attested. "Pvt. Brown was killed during this attack."

Scotty Brown had the sad distinction of being the only Cape Codder killed at Pearl Harbor, and in the coming months, many letters of condolence and posthumous awards came to his mother. "It may be comforting to you to know of the high esteem in which he has always been held by everyone in Chatham," wrote Carl Anderson, commander of Chatham Post 253 of the American Legion. Mrs. Ayers also received letters from Massachusetts governor Leverett Saltonstall and U.S. senator Henry Cabot Lodge.

Scotty "was one of the swellest fellows you could ever meet," said his friend Frederick E. Rogers, a local accountant and the brother of artist Wendell Rogers.[10]

"As you know, I am pretty much by myself here at home and in my work," Wendell wrote to Mrs. Ayers two weeks after Scotty's death. "I have often sensed the presence of dear ones on the other side and am more and more convinced as time goes on, that there is but a thin veil between us." He advised Scotty's mother to think of Scotty still on the other side of the world, in Hawaii, happy in what he is doing.

When Charlotte Forgeron heard about Scotty's death, she remembered his promise to send her an alligator. Now it was too late.[11]

With Scotty's death, everything had changed—not just for Mrs. Ayers and his friends in Chatham but also for the world.

BEFORE THE WAR: MINNIE BUCK

By the end of the Great Depression, Chatham had turned into a hardscrabble town. Long known as a fishing village, that profession was a tough way to earn a living, and many fathers counseled their sons to find other work. For those who chose to fish, the lucky ones were those who loved working outdoors on the salt water in the cold, biting air and for whom fishing was a calling.

Although people said you'd never starve in Chatham during the Depression—you could always dig up some clams or catch some fish—life was, nonetheless, hard. By the spring of 1940, tourism had become the most lucrative game in town. The town's position on the elbow of Cape Cod, with water on three sides, coupled with its downright beauty, gave it tremendous advantages for catching the tourist trade. Still, life wasn't easy, even for an educated professional woman like dentist Minnie Buck.

Wartime at Home

On one particular day in May 1940, with the war still something being fought far away, some say that Minnie Buck descended into the small, round Cape Cod cellar to fetch a jar of homemade preserves from the stock she stored down there. As a widow whose only daughter had married and moved far away, Minnie often welcomed female lodgers into the large, rambling house just off Main Street where she had practiced dentistry for nearly forty years.

The cellar was reached either through a trapdoor that opened from the floor of the dining room, exposing a ladder, or through an outdoor bulkhead that revealed a set of brick stairs. The bulkhead and trapdoor were probably equidistant from the kitchen, where, late in the day, Minnie and a lodger, Blanche Reynolds, might have been preparing a plate of buttered bread, which, it suddenly seemed, would be much improved by a smear of homemade beach plum jam.

Many people—especially a woman of nearly seventy-two, wearing a dress reaching well below her knees and perhaps wary of breaking a bone—might shy away from the perilous ladder down which one descended backward into the cellar's gloom. Still, Minnie knew the house; she had scampered up and down the ladder since she was a girl of twelve. She might have chosen either the indoor or outdoor route.

The snug cellar itself was only about ten feet in diameter and lined with bricks. Said to be Dutch in origin, the round cellars offered no corners for mold or for spiders to spin their webs. "Old timers said that witches and ghosts would not stay where there were no corners to hide in."[12] Windowless, the only light oozed in through either the open bulkhead or the trapdoor. These days, Minnie's eyes did not adjust as quickly to the dark as they once had. Searching for the glass jar of preserves, which stood on a table, she struck a match.

When the explosion rocked the neighborhood, some residents may have feared that the distant war in Europe had finally come to Chatham. It was May 23, 1940, the day of the first great dogfight between Spitfire airplanes in the skies above England. German tanks had just forced their way into Atrecht, France, and also captured the Port of Boulogne. While the United States was not yet at war, front-page headline news from Europe was uniformly grim.

The explosion tore the northern side of the 1828 Greek revival house from its foundation, blew out doors and windows, shot shards of glass fifty yards, shattered plaster walls and ripped right up into the dining room, where it "tossed about heavy articles." Neighbors later said the blast sounded like "a huge chest of dishes landing from a great height."[13]

The snug, round Cape Cod cellar where seventy-two-year-old dentist Minnie Buck was fatally injured in a gas explosion in May 1940. It holds no dark secrets. *Photo by the author.*

Minnie, with her face, hands, arms and legs badly burned, staggered in her singed and tattered dress partway upstairs, most likely following the narrow brick stairs leading to the outdoors. The force of the explosion would have blasted off the door to the bulkhead, and the brick steps would have provided an easier exit than the wooden ladder, which may have been destroyed in the explosion. Blanche Reynolds met her halfway up the stairs and helped her out.

The newspapers called what happened in the basement of the house on the corner of Cross Street and Shattuck Place a "freak gas explosion." The strange thing was that Minnie's house was not connected to the gas line. It was assumed that gas had entered the basement from the Shattuck Place line through a water pipe that had sprung a leak.

Although the fire department was summoned, nothing was burning.

Neighbors later told investigators that they had smelled a strong gas odor in their own cellars. Why hadn't Minnie smelled gas? And if she did smell gas, why did she strike that match?

Minnie Buck was christened Marinda Gifford. Standing four feet, ten inches when full grown, she took the nickname Minnie. By 1940, Minnie was said to have been one of the oldest women practicing dentistry in the country. She became very active in the Cape Cod District (Dental) Society starting in 1933, when the group was formed, and took particular interest in encouraging children to care for their teeth.

Minnie's patients most likely entered the office through a door on the Shattuck Place side of the house. The door still has an old-fashioned brass bell that you twist to ring. The patients waited for her in a room next to the dining room. The room where Minnie practiced her dental arts was on the south side of the house, and already in the 1930s, she might have built out the bay window. Sitting in the dental chair in that nook on a sunny morning, her patients would be bathed in sunlight and, with their heads tilted back, could enjoy a view of the sky and trees—as the sunshine illuminated their teeth.

Minnie was so small that, the story goes, she sometimes sat in the laps of her larger male patients as she probed and filled their teeth. When drilling, Minnie stood beside the chair and, with her foot, worked a treadle that powered the drill—an awe- or fear-inspiring piece of equipment driven by pullies. Although dental drills had been electrified, Minnie's house probably did not have electricity until about 1920, and even then, for many years service would be erratic.

A few minutes after the explosion, Reggie Nickerson, a fourteen-year-old student at Chatham High, trundled around the corner of Cross Street with his father, who was driving a laundry truck. Minnie was by now lying on the lawn. It was a cool day for May, with temperatures in the upper forties; the sky was overcast, and it had been raining a little. Reggie watched from the window of the truck as Mrs. Howes from across Cross Street bent over Minnie, holding her hand.[14] Behind them, the side of the house looked like a picture from war-torn Europe. Just then, the old vehicle that served as an ambulance rattled up Cross Street from the Eldredge Garage. Blanche Reynolds had summoned Dr. Benjamin Keene—Doc Keene, as everyone called him—whose home office was around the corner on Seaview Street, and he performed first aid at the scene. Doc Keene oversaw the loading of Minnie into the ambulance. The district nurse, Marion McNeece, attended Minnie in the ambulance en route to Cape Cod Hospital in Hyannis, a facility that had been open for twenty years.

Minnie's neighborhood was home to people engaged in a mix of professions; until his death in 1938, Charles Howes had lived a few doors down in a pretty Gothic revival house. Howes was a sailmaker whom a local artist, Fred Wight, had painted in oils. Also on the street were Sewell Marks, principal of the high school, and Ernie Eldredge and his son, Desmond, both fishermen. Another neighbor kept a summertime hotel, and yet another worked as an operator at the local radio company.

Just around the corner, on a small farm on Shattuck Place, lived Minnie's good friend Alice Guild (pronounced to rhyme with "wild"). Mrs. Guild had written the Chatham column in the *Chatham Monitor*—a newspaper that covered events Cape-wide—for several decades.[15] Mrs. Guild, who was born in 1876, was seven and a half years younger than Minnie and had arrived in Chatham as a married woman, in 1909, the same year Minnie's daughter was born. The women became friends and collaborated in 1911 in founding the Chatham Reading Club, a group designed to foster the intellectual interests of Chatham's women and busy young mothers. In 1923, they again collaborated in founding the Chatham Historical Society, and the pair was instrumental in raising money to purchase the 1752 Atwood House, a rare

The Guild farm on Shattuck Place in the late 1930s. Visible are a chicken coop and a well house. "What a magical place," Minnie Buck's granddaughter remembered. Alice Guild had a green thumb that extended to begonias on her sun porch. *Photo courtesy of Gene Guild.*

Dentist Minnie Buck died of burns and shock in 1940, twenty-four hours after a violent gas explosion in her old Cape Cod cellar. She was buried in her husband's family plot in South Chatham. *Photo by the author.*

gambrel-roofed structure believed to be the oldest in town. They also worked closely restoring it themselves.[16]

After a night at the hospital, Minnie died. About twenty-four hours had passed since the explosion in her cellar. The cause of death was listed as second-degree burns and "shock." Minnie's daughter, Josephine, was married and living in Kansas with her own daughter. The following week, after a funeral at the Universalist church, Minnie was buried at the South Chatham cemetery. The day Minnie died, her glass jars of preserves were found intact, standing on the table in the cellar where they had stood before the explosion. Her goldfish, too, survived the explosion in a glass bowl "almost hidden beneath debris" in the dining room.

THE WAY IT WAS, 1940

"A secluded Summer house, overlooking Pleasant Bay," was on offer in the *New York Times.* It had seven bedrooms, two baths, a coal range, an electric refrigerator, 435 feet of beachfront and an available handyman. "Restricted. References required." It was a bargain at $700 for the season, but Jews and "ethnic types" were not wanted.[17] The town's one minority family, the James family from Gay Head, had a tough time. As one recalled, "You get to the point where you don't stick out your little brown hand, because you don't want it slapped anymore."[18]

Chatham was not alone, of course, in its discriminatory attitudes. "Although polite people did not talk about it, anti-Semitism grew significantly in the United States during this time, especially with the prominence of so many Jews in the Roosevelt administration."[19]

Interestingly, in a town where the hotels and rentals restricted Jewish guests, one of the most eminent citizens was now-retired Justice Louis Brandeis, whose family had been vacationing in Chatham since 1924, when the justice bought an antique double Cape house in a secluded area off Cedar Street near Oyster River. "The life style of Louis Brandeis, his deep love of simplicity, is accurately reflected in this Cape Cod house," which is "modest, sturdy" and "forthright."[20] The justice usually spent the entire summer in Chatham, entertaining illustrious persons and working on legal papers, and returned to Washington, D.C., in time for the court's reconvening on the first Monday in October.[21]

Now that he had retired, "he will walk a little, enjoy the garden and the sight of surf on Chatham bar, will motor quite a good deal," reported the *New York Times*.[22] Favorite pastimes for Brandeis and his wife, Alice, had always been canoeing, walking, picking wild blueberries and visiting with their children and four grandchildren.

Yet Brandeis had not left the world stage. Sometime around 1940, Brandeis hosted a small summit of Zionists at his home.[23] A photograph shows Brandeis and Alice standing on the porch with eight men in suits identified as "Zionist leaders." "Few people at first took seriously the rise of Adolph Hitler and Nazism," Brandeis's biographer wrote.

The war was still far off. On Main Street, "band concerts each Friday evening are drawing the usual crowd and making traffic a slow affair for a little while on that evening," Alice Guild noted.[24] Doc Keene played the French horn in the band.[25]

By August, when Mary Winslow's *Private Lives* was playing at the Monomoy Theatre, "nothing could be more welcome than the cool breeze which sprang up Wednesday noon," Guild wrote in the *Monitor*.

Members of the First Congregational Church took up a special offering to help the thousands of homeless refugees of the war in Europe.

"Aid [Europe] in a material way? Certainly, so far as knitting and sewing and charitable work were concerned; 'Bundles for Britain' societies were organized, or being organized, in most of Ostable County's towns," wrote Joseph Lincoln.[26] With the memory of the Great War still fresh, Lincoln summed up the prevailing mood in America before the invasion of Pearl Harbor: "We might conceivably be forced into war, but even if we were—a very remote chance—no expeditionary force of young Americans should again cross the ocean to fight Europe's battles for her, no sir!"

Wartime at Home

THE WAR CREEPS CLOSER

On January 2, 1941, the *Chatham Monitor* printed a photo of a swastika hanging in Paris, with the Eiffel Tower clearly visible in the background. Yet also on page one of that first *Monitor* of 1941 was an article headlined "The Cape Looks Forward." The thrust of the story was that while army soldiers would be in training at Camp Edwards, twenty-five miles away near the Cape Cod Canal, the business sector should consider that some fifteen hundred soldiers would be on daily leave from the camp. "Our business is to accommodate the visiting public," the article said. "Everyone who can afford it has a right to come to the Cape and enjoy it."

And in fact, although twenty-seven thousand soldiers were housed at Camp Edwards, they did not disrupt life on Cape Cod.[27] Traffic at the canal had been speeded up with the 1935 opening of the Bourne and Sagamore Bridges and improved roadwork in the area.

The Cape's summer business had doubled in the past ten years, putting the estimated revenue of the Cape's recreation at $20 million. "All in all we are entering upon an extremely interesting decade and it will certainly witness plenty of action," the article predicted in what might later be read as a grotesque understatement.[28]

During the Great War, a Naval Air Station had been built in Chatham Port on Nickerson's Neck. Now a persistent rumor rumbled that the U.S. government would establish a sea- and land-plane base "on a large and very modern scale" with immense underground hangars on the same site. "The site, favored by a harbor and giving immediate access to the ocean, is regarded as well suited for the locating of planes for reconnoitering or defense purposes," Alice Guild wrote in the *Monitor*.[29]

Rumors had it that "dredges will arrive this week to improve the basin by the field. Most people are waiting to see before believing." Men approached David Bangs, an instructor at the Chatham Flying Club, looking for work. Perhaps fueling the rumors was the partial cleanup of the base in March 1939, when newspapers carried a photo of the enormous hangar before and after it was pulled down. "The roof of the hangar came gently to earth, cushioned by air."[30] The selectmen, however, said they knew nothing about any such plans, and they weren't being coy—no such plans ever materialized.

Meanwhile, Guild noted that Z. Clinton Kendrick was stricken with a hemorrhage on Main Street. He was carried into the Eldredge Public Library, "where he passed away immediately." Yet despite tuberculosis,

This rare photograph helps answer one mystery of how Chatham's northern Twin Light was moved to Eastham in 1923. The photo, by light keeper James T. Allison, shows that the five-ring lighthouse was dismantled. How the pieces were moved remains a mystery. *Photo courtesy of the Chatham, Massachusetts Historical Society.*

scarlet fever and even smallpox, the average age of death in Chatham was sixty-seven compared to the national average of sixty-two.

On March 13, 1941, Dr. Frank Bertell Worthing died at age seventy. Less than a year earlier, townspeople had celebrated Dr. Worthing's birthday with a big hoopla. He received over one hundred greeting cards from all around the country, and the impressionist painter Harold Dunbar painted an enormous card called *The Three Landmarks*. The landmarks were Chatham Light—now a single light, as its twin was moved to Eastham in 1923—the Old Mill and Dr. Worthing.

Dr. Worthing's seventieth birthday also marked thirty-six years since he saw his first patient in Chatham. He began his career as a physician, dentist and druggist, making house calls on a horse and buggy. He once traveled twenty miles over the sand to deliver a baby on Monomoy Point, and during his career he delivered one set of triplets and many twins. In recent years, he had scaled back his practice by declining night calls and obstetrical cases. He was a well-known figure, often seen standing outside his Main Street house, next door to the busy post office on the corner of Chatham Bars Avenue and Main Street. There he declaimed on many topics, including town politics, and even indulged in a few "sidewalk consultations."[31]

With the deaths of Dr. Worthing and Dr. Buck, medicine had moved into the hands of a younger generation.

YOKELS IN FAIRYLAND

The summer of 1941 was not much different from previous summers. "In a peaceful little world of its own Cape Cod is going ahead with its vacation plans. The war has failed to interfere with the recreation program of this peninsula."[32]

An article was published on July 23, 1941, in the *Boston Herald* under the headline "Chatham Satisfied with Simple Life." In interviews with novelist Joseph Lincoln; Harold Dunbar, who also published a magazine; Mary Winslow, "socialite, owner, scene designer and 'handy man'" of the Monomoy Theatre; muralist Alice Stallknecht; Selectman Edwin Kidder; and "shipwreck connoisseur" George Bloomer, the paper offered a succinct view of Chatham.

"Here the city dweller finds something like a fairyland, its narrow lanes aglow with rambler roses and flowering privet hedges and its air heavy with scents of land and sea," wrote *Herald* reporter Lawrence Dame.

Dame spoke first with Lincoln, who assured him that life on the Cape was now dull compared to the good old days when the town sent its young men to sea. Dunbar then resurrected his old joke of June 1937 that Chatham secede and become the Cod Island Republic, with Dunbar acting as "supreme coderator."[33]

Dame also rehashed the story of the controversy over Stallknecht's murals in the First Congregational Church. In *Christ Preaching to the Multitude* and *The Circle Supper*, Stallknecht had used members of the church as models. The two enormous murals now hung in the church itself and had become tourist attractions. Voluntary donations had helped the church pay for a new furnace and shingle the west roof.

The winter population of Chatham (2,136, according to the 1940 census) tripled in the summer, and Kidder boasted that "summer residents pay

62 percent of every tax dollar—and like it." One blot on the horizon of this Eden was the government's proposal to take over the ten-mile-long peninsula of Monomoy—an issue that just would not die. Monomoy was a favorite camping and hunting spot, an inexpensive, nearby getaway for all of Chatham's residents. A zoning law, too, had been defeated three times, but Kidder predicted it would rise again.

Kidder, an avid bird hunter and fisherman, served as president of the Lower Cape Surfcasters Club. Surfcasting, a relatively recent sport, was taking hold, especially at Monomoy.

In fobbing off his account of quaint Chatham, one wonders how many of Dame's readers realize that, of his six informants, only one, George Bloomer, is a native of Chatham. Four, in fact, came from off Cape. It is as though the point of view of a Cape Codder cannot possibly be fathomed.[34]

AN INEXPLICABLE MURDER

If something evil was in the zeitgeist during the summer of 1941, Frances G. Rogers was feeling it. The forty-nine-year-old mother, a life member of the Order of the Eastern Star and a worshipper at the Chatham Methodist Church, may have been experiencing the depression of menopause. Or perhaps she had a chronic illness. In any event, she had been under the care of a doctor "for some time." And with the Great Depression barely over, money was probably tight.[35]

It was shortly before 9:00 a.m. at the very end of July. The summer season was at its peak. Less than four weeks earlier, the town had, as usual, celebrated the Fourth of July with a parade and festivities, despite the war in Europe. A few days earlier, a fifty-piece band from Camp Edwards had joined stunt flyers in an event to raise money for a RAF Flying Ambulance. Harold Dunbar was among those donating art to be auctioned.[36]

On this particular morning, as her only child, Thomas, a boy of twelve, slept in the back bedroom of the family home on Main Street, Mrs. Rogers entered the room and whacked him on the head with a hammer. When he was unconscious, Mrs. Rogers knotted an electrical cord taut around his neck and tied it to the bedpost. The boy never struggled as she stuffed his nose and mouth with cotton.

Mrs. Rogers unsuccessfully tried to commit suicide. She was remanded to a psychiatric hospital in Taunton as the court decided what to do with her.

THE DEATH OF A JUSTICE

In August 1941, the town considered allocating $2,000 for a fish packinghouse.[37] And on August 11, George M. Haskins, publisher of four weekly newspapers, including the *Chatham Monitor*, died after a long illness.[38] His death was perhaps also the death knell for the *Monitor*, founded in 1871, which would fold within two years. On October 5, Justice Brandeis died in Washington, D.C. During the previous summer in Chatham, he had suffered from a bout of pneumonia. On October 1, seemingly on the mend, he suffered a heart attack.

"Justice Brandeis was recognized as one of America's greatest defenders of the value of the single human individual and the value of freedom of choice."[39]

During the fall, "more and more young men were called into service," Joseph Lincoln wrote in his final wartime novel.[40] "Uniforms, of one kind or another, were frequently seen along Main Street."

WAVES OF CHANGE: AFTER PEARL HARBOR

During that week before the Japanese invaded Pearl Harbor, Chatham native Joe Nickerson was working as a carpenter "for a fellow in Harwich" at seventy-five cents an hour. On Sunday, he drove up to Braintree to visit his fiancée, Louise Wentworth, whom he was planning to marry in February. With the unseasonably warm weather, it was nice to get out and about. Joe was listening to music on the radio when an announcer broke in at about 2:30 p.m. with the first news of the invasion. "I said, 'There goes our wedding all to pieces,'" Nickerson later reminisced.[41]

The Japanese invasion of Pearl Harbor marked the end of America's innocence. As of December 8, the United States was at war, and life in Chatham would switch gears. Ocean waves had attracted tourists while providing a bounty for the fishing industry; now, radio waves offered new and challenging uses. Waves of change rippled through Chatham.

During the weeks after December 7, men from the U.S. Navy arrived in Chatham and commandeered the radio station in the Marconi buildings in Chatham Port. During the Great War, too, the government had taken over the buildings that the Marconi Corporation had erected in 1914 and run its own secret military communications center there. After the war, RCA bought and ran the station, WCC (Wireless Cape Cod), a transmitting and receiving station for marine traffic that was often in the national spotlight.

In 1914, the Marconi Corporation established a radio station in Chatham Port. During World War II, the navy took over the station to intercept U-boat signals using an antenna pointed to Berlin. This radio tower is at Ryder's Cove, across from the Marconi campus. *Photo by the author.*

The Arctic explorer Richard Byrd and pilots Charles Lindbergh and Amelia Earhart relied on the station for accurate weather briefings.

During World War II, the navy-run station was referred to as Chatham Station C. It played an important wartime role in detecting, locating and intercepting intelligence of German U-boats and aircraft.

Until new tactics and technology appeared during the second half of the sixty-nine-month Battle of the Atlantic, the sole defense against the U-boat was avoidance. Chatham Station C, intercepting U-boat traffic, enabled convoys to know the whereabouts and intentions of German U-boats and thus avoid attack. The role of Chatham Station C in saving lives and vessels, although unsung, is highly significant.

Claude W. "Dick" Lumpkin, chief in charge of Teletypes for the U.S. Navy, worked in the station directing the men teletypewriting secret coded enemy communications with ships and submarines. A couple of miles away, a heavily defended Army Air Forces radar station was established on Great Hill; there, men ran a manually operated decimeter aircraft radar. SPARS, the women's division of the Coast Guard, ran a LORAN station at Chatham Light while the Coast Guard patrolled the coast.

Eleven registered nurses signed up to run the first aid post in the Chatham school. "Five beach wagons are already available for use as ambulances," the *Cape Cod Standard-Times* reported on December 11, 1941. "Eleven panel trucks will be at the disposal of the organization."

The plans of Chatham's men and women were disrupted. Before the invasion of Pearl Harbor, Joe Nickerson had tried to enlist in the army but was declared 4-F due to high blood pressure. Now, however, physical requirements for troops were less strict. He was accepted into the navy in May 1942 and served as a first class carpenter. Eventually, he was sent to Guam, where he helped build Fleet Hospital 115.[42]

DON'T LET THEM SEE US OR HEAR US

It was wartime, and the telephone company urged its customers to be discreet. Who might be listening in? During the two weeks after Roosevelt declared war, wartime regulations began that would profoundly affect civilian life.

At the end of 1941, Chatham hotels, which, after nearly three decades of tourism, were efficient establishments, found themselves refitting with four bunks to a room to house military personnel. Even Chatham's fishermen were photographed and fingerprinted.[43] The police department acquired new duties fingerprinting defense workers and investigating their records, as well as those of all applying for the armed forces.

"World War II, with its gas rationing and the bustle of a nation more concerned with victory than vacations, slowed tourism to a trickle and once more brought down the price of Cape Cod property."[44] Tourism was put on hold.

The Office of Civilian Defense took out a full-page ad titled "What to Do in an Air Raid" in the *Chatham Monitor* on December 18. Instructions were to keep cool, stay home, put out lights, lie down and stay away from windows. "You can help lick the Japs, with your bare hands, if you will just do these few, simple things."

. The air raid wardens and their deputies patrolled the town to ensure that residents followed blackout rules. Blankets, tar paper, oil cloth, wall board and heavy, dark draperies were all acceptable methods to cover windows to prevent any light from escaping from a house. While electricity would remain on, houses must lie in total blackness.

In *The Bradshaws of Harniss*, Joseph Lincoln's character Jacob Lemon, a ne'er-do-well who always knew which way the wind was blowing, became a local air raid warden. "No one was more alert than he to detect a spark of light beneath the drawn window-shades of his neighbor on blackout nights."[45] Eventually, Lemon gets his comeuppance after he accepts a ten-dollar bribe from a weekender at whose seaside house he continuously reported seeing lights leaking out.

The upper half of the headlights on cars were painted black to prevent their glow from being seen from the sky.

Lighthouses raised interesting issues during the war. While the coastline, especially around Chatham, was so perilous that twin lights were first erected in 1806, the beams of lighthouses would clearly give the enemy the same guidance as they gave the fishermen.[46]

"Chatham Light was one of the few American lighthouses to remain in service during World War II, testifying to its importance," wrote lighthouse expert Jeremy D'Entremont.[47] Summer visitor Elinor Miller recalled a room

"Chatham Light was one of the few American lighthouses to remain in service during World War II, testifying to its importance," writes lighthouse expert Jeremy D'Entremont. Here, it is decorated for Christmas. *Photo by the author.*

her parents rented at the head of Bridge Street during the war. "I would lie awake at night and count the flashes of the Chatham Light as it sent its beams seaward."[48]

Slim Hutchings called a public meeting at the school hall, where shifts of female volunteers worked at an air raid station, to acquaint people with what they might do in an emergency. Applicants to the navy needed at least eighteen "natural, serviceable teeth," with a minimum of two molars in functional occlusion.[49]

The year ended with a nod to Christmas as the Chatham Band sponsored a carol sing in Kate Gould Park. Rain forced the event into the Methodist church, where over three hundred people crowded in to sing under the direction of Percy Atwood. Reconditioned toys were taken to the Legion Hall for distribution to needy children.[50]

Oscar Doane chaired the committee on public safety. The initial 300 workers under him had dropped to 160 when 140 of them enlisted. Early in 1942, Doane was busy testing the town's alarm system when he discovered that it could not be clearly heard throughout the town. He set about remedying that.

Margaret Guild, ANC

"My cute little, fat little, red headed sister," began a letter to fifteen-year-old Margaret Elinor Guild from one of her older brothers. "I am glad to hear that you have a dog as the lack of any animal on the place would be an omission unworthy of the spirit surrounding so complete a collection," her brother (who signed the letter Julius Seesher—no doubt a joke on "seashore") wrote from Somerville. "Julius" concludes the letter with a sketch of a short, rotund female figure in a bathing cap standing on a pier. "Your fellow" has just jumped off the end of the pier and is represented by a pair of feet sticking out of the water.[51]

Margaret, who would joke right back with anyone who joshed her about her weight, tucked the letter into a scrapbook she kept covering the first three decades of her life.

Margaret was the youngest of the five living children of Charles and Alice Guild. Born in 1908 in Keene, New Hampshire, Margaret moved to Chatham with her family in 1910. (Alice originally came to Chatham as a teacher; Charles served as high school superintendent.) Margaret graduated in the Chatham High School class of 1926 with Virginia Harding. The class's motto was: "We have crossed the Bay, the Ocean lies before us."

Margaret Guild, World War II army nurse. In the decades after the war, Guild would become a driving force in the health of Chatham's adults and children. A modest woman, she nearly did not attend her own retirement party. *Photo courtesy of the Chatham, Massachusetts Historical Society.*

The following fall, Margaret crossed not a bay but the Cape Cod Canal and enrolled in the Massachusetts Homeopathic Hospital School of Nursing, from which she graduated in 1929. Margaret is "short—stout—not over neat," an instructor wrote. Also "good natured, easy going, kindly by nature—always willing to please."

During the early 1930s, she roomed with other nurses on Huntington Avenue in Boston and continued to work at the hospital. Some days she assisted with up to four surgeries, including appendectomies, colostomies, Caesarians and the amputation of limbs. In 1932, she acquired her first driver's license, and in 1934, she heard a performance of Wagner's *Götterdämmerung* in the nearby Boston Opera House. Her brother Bernard was also an opera lover. That same year, she was invited to the wedding of Josephine Buck, the daughter of her mother's good friend Minnie Buck. Margaret and Josephine, just a year apart in age, had grown up within a few houses of each other and were best friends.

In the late 1930s, Margaret moved back home to Chatham and into the Shattuck Place house where her parents still lived. Margaret's nephew

Gene Guild describes her as a "firm, stubborn, take-charge" person who would watch the health of family members and even offer her blood for a transfusion if necessary.[52]

On Pearl Harbor Day, Margaret perhaps remembered the example of her older half sister Helen, who had served as a nurse for six months in France during the Great War. Thirty-three-year-old Margaret enlisted in the U.S. Army Nurse Corps and was stationed at Camp Edwards.

LONNIE PICKETT SR.

Early in 1942, Lonnie Pickett Sr., who served as a radar technician in the Army Air Corps, was stationed at an Army Air Forces radar station up on Great Hill by the water towers. There the army maintained barracks, storage buildings and the radar tower itself, high up on the hill. Machine gun emplacements protected the unit. Pickett's job was at the guardhouse down at the entrance to the facility.

Although details are scarce, the radar is believed to be an SCR 270 radar unit taken from a Signal Corps depot perhaps in Boston or Fort Monmouth. The Signal Corps was a pioneer in the radar field and researched, developed

Lonnie Pickett Sr. (right) wields a Thompson submachine gun as he guards the Army Air Forces radar facility on Great Hill during World War II. With him is John Miller. A decade later, Pickett made his home near the site. *Photo courtesy of Lonnie Pickett Jr.*

and contracted out the production of its own equipment. Its equipment was state of the art, and the newest unit, the SCR 270, was already being deployed to such remote locations as Hawaii, Panama and Iceland when the war broke out. (In fact, it was an SCR 270 located at Opana on Oahu that reported the subsequently disregarded signal of approaching Japanese aircraft during the invasion of Pearl Harbor.)

Pickett met his future wife, Evelyn Bearse, in Chatham. Before the war, Evelyn had typed Joseph Lincoln's manuscripts. Soon after their marriage, Pickett was transferred to the Cadillac Mountain Radar site in Bar Harbor, Maine, where Lonnie Jr. was born in 1943, and then to San Antonio, Texas.[53]

On February 17, at the annual town meeting, a resolution regarding the death of Scotty Brown brought townspeople to their feet. "We will receive him back again, wrapped in the flag for whose honor and defense he fought so bravely and fell so nobly, soon to fill the patriot's grave." In April, between three hundred and four hundred people filled the Methodist church to capacity at Brown's memorial service.

1942: WEDDING BELLS, A BABY, SABOTEURS AND FEAR

On March 2, 1942, a Victory Market, the brainchild of Mrs. Francis B. Shaw, opened on Main Street. Sales at the store would raise money for the war effort.

On April 10, Harold Dunbar, who at age fifty-nine was too old to serve in the military, married Florence Gertrude Bower Buck, age thirty-six, known as Gertrude. Dunbar's first marriage to Dorothy Brownstein, "Brownie," had unofficially ended when Brownie left him in 1923 and officially ended ten years later when Brownie died.

In the March 1938 issue of the *Cape Cod Beacon*, Dunbar had written about himself, under the pseudonym Letty the Old-timer, "This man, the coward, runs away from women, and tries to muddle along by himself. He says no woman would have him, anyway, and I guess he may be right. Anyway, I'd be sorry for the woman who did." Yet in Gertrude he did find a woman who would.

Gertrude's marriage to Harold was a second marriage for her, also. Her first husband was a local architect, and it seems that Harold and Gertrude may have discovered their mutual attraction while working together in the amateur theatre that Harold had established in a defunct toy factory. (The theatre later became Mary Winslow's Monomoy, which, in turn, was taken over by the University of Ohio Players in 1958 after Elizabeth Baker, wife of the president of that university, bought it.) Or perhaps they flirted over a bowl of quahog stew in Gertrude's Little Chowder Shanty, which was in "a picturesque place of hills and sand and quiet water" away from the main part of town.[54] The couple would begin their married life in Harold's new house on Sunset Lane in the heart of Chatham's Old Village.

Alice Stallknecht became a grandmother early in the summer of 1942, on June 24, when her grandson George Frederic Wight was born. The baby's mother was Joan Elizabeth Bingham, whom Alice's son Fred had married in 1936. At the start of the war, Alice's murals were still on display in the Congregational church. "The three paintings, each of which averages about 15 feet square, have been an attraction for Summer visitors and a source of pride for Chatham residents since they embellished the church walls."[55]

The writer Robert Nathan spent the summer of 1942 about thirty miles up the road from Chatham, in Truro. Truro, like Chatham, was the site of an early Marconi radio station; Truro, like Chatham, would later be the site of a Cold War radar facility.

In his novel *Journal for Josephine*, Nathan captures the strange, stressful air of that summer. In the spring, birds return and build nests as they always do; on the other hand, Nathan serves as an air spotter and is told he can no longer use binoculars on the beach. "A notice from the Chief of Police, to say that the police are taking over the enforcement of the dim-out, and that black shades must be used at all windows," he wrote.[56] "But the police cannot put out the lighthouse light which shines sixty miles to sea." ("Sixty miles to sea" was, of course, an exaggeration.)

Nathan referred to Highland Light, Cape Cod's first light, built in 1797 over Peaked Hill Bars about a mile off the northeast coast of the Cape.[57]

During a blackout test, "the lighthouse light roamed through the sky as usual, and fireflies made arrowy lanterns in the air," Nathan wrote.[58] When the siren signaled the end of the test, "we put on our lights, and brought out some beer."

In Truro, the rumor mill came into play as it did in Chatham. Someone said that "parachute troops may drop in on us at any moment—though what they would gain by that, I cannot imagine, unless Germany has her eyes on our beach-plum jelly," he wrote.[59] "Still, it would be a simple thing for a U-boat to put a number of men ashore, at night, in a rowboat, with orders to pick up a hostage or two, or just to burn a few houses."

After a German U-boat dropped saboteurs on Long Island in June 1942, paranoia crested along the East Coast. "People have no idea how much fear there was around here," Chatham fisherman Dave Ryder said.[60] The Coast Guard patrolled Chatham's Atlantic shoreline with dogs.

A WHOLE NEW WORLD AT WAR

The year 1942 was, in some ways, the most fearful for Americans, with many people expecting bombs to fall on American cities. In truth, the war was being fought not far off the East Coast. At the beginning of the war, the United States was ill prepared, particularly when Admiral Dönitz launched "Operation *Paukenschlag*" (drumbeat) in December 1941. For the next several months,

The class of 1946 poses on the steps of the old school on Main Street. During the war, the school doubled as a first aid post, and students followed a special wartime curriculum that included commando courses and patriotic songs. *Photo courtesy of the Chatham, Massachusetts Historical Society.*

Wartime at Home

Dönitz's U-boats targeted tankers and American ships from Maine to North Carolina.[61] One summer resident remembers that her family kept lighter fluid in the car to clean the tar off their feet after swimming at Hardings Beach. The tar was said to have washed up from tankers sunk off the East Coast.[62]

Meanwhile, the British were working round-the-clock to break the naval Enigma code, which the Germans had made more complex.

When school resumed at Chatham High that fall, students entered a new wartime program. During their junior and senior years, boys went through a pre-induction Victory Corps Program. Fourteen boys were enrolled in preflight aeronautics. Commando courses were offered to both boys and girls in all the grades.

In her annual report, Miss Eleanor Anifantis, who taught music, stressed that "stirring patriotic songs make our children conscious of what we hold dear and of the task that lies before us. Let's sing our way to Victory."[63]

Young people conducted scrap metal drives. In November 1942, the Young People's Society of the Methodist church won $100 from the *Standard-Times* for turning in the most metal salvage on the Cape. The government asked that 20 percent of all school typewriters be given to the government for defense use. The school department handed over two.

HOME FIRES CHATHAM

In October 1942, Mrs. Edna Matteson began a monthly newsletter called *Home Fires* to keep Chatham's soldiers informed about the doings back home. Subtitled "Greetings from Chatham to Be Issued Once a Month," Mrs. Matteson took it upon herself to write a two-page roundup of local news, cramming in as many names as possible in good local newspaper style. She then mailed her newsletter to a growing list of Chatham's men and women serving in the armed forces both in the United States and abroad. As she wrote in September 1944, at the start of her third year with the newsletter, "My one hope is that through that time, you have been able to close your eyes and sort of walk down town and got a bit of the news and gossip."[64]

Matteson was herself a mother of two servicemen. She was a well-known figure who had joined the Ladies Reading Club in the 1920s, and she sometimes sang solos at events at the Congregational church. Hired in the 1930s to patrol the restroom at the bureau of tourism building, she energetically responded to 450 letters of inquiry in 1938 alone. She seemed to be a woman with much initiative and drive.

Her newsletter, which ran through June 1945, provides a colorful snapshot of the town's doings, particularly after the *Chatham Monitor* folded in 1943. Matteson's writing style is vivid, with much of her news conveyed in the form of breathless announcements separated by hyphens. She mixes homely news with wartime zingers that alerted those who were away that life was not the same even in those most familiar places.

"The summer season was not very successful, the stores doing about 75 percent of usual business, Hotels closed early," Matteson wrote. "Stage Harbor Yacht Club held races for women and children. Charity sales at the Victory Market were up, though."

Mrs. Matteson failed to mention that Halloween 1942 was marred by hooliganism. Thirty-two street signs, thirty-two lanterns and torches were taken.[65]

In November, coffee rationing began.

DON'T MESS WITH SPARS

"I didn't even know what a lighthouse was," Petty Officer Second Class Anita Freeman[66] said many years later, describing her arrival in Chatham to work at the Coast Guard's Long Range Aid to Navigation (LORAN) facility at Chatham Light. Freeman was twenty-four, a native of Detroit and Cleveland and a long way from the Midwest.[67]

Late in 1942, a LORAN station opened at the Coast Guard station by the Chatham Light. Eleven SPARS—the women's division of the Coast Guard, derived from the Coast Guard motto *semper paratus*—were soon running the station and living there.[68] Station Chatham, Unit 21, was under the command of Lieutenant Vera Hamerschlag. (The commanding officer of the station itself was Edwin Kidder, who in 1942 left the board of selectmen.) Unit 21 is believed to have been the only all-female monitoring station of its kind in the world.[69]

LORAN was a navigation technology invented by Alfred Loomis, a millionaire patron of physicists and owner of a first-class laboratory at Tuxedo Park, New York.[70]

After the LORAN project was transferred to MIT's radiation laboratory in 1942, it was improved to increase range and accuracy. In 1942, stations were set up in Nova Scotia, Newfoundland, Labrador and Greenland, as well as in Duluth, Minnesota, and on Cape Cod to form an east–west baseline. A chain of stations began operations in 1943, and the U.S. Coast Guard assumed control that same year.

"I didn't even know what a lighthouse was," Petty Officer Second Class Anita Freeman said, describing her arrival in Chatham to work at the Coast Guard's LORAN facility at Chatham Light. Freeman was twenty-four and a long way from home. *Photo by the author.*

In Chatham, the SPARS in Unit 21 monitored LORAN signals twenty-four hours a day. The signals were picked up by a 250-foot antenna behind the Coast Guard station. Inside a monitoring room with black-painted walls, the SPARS recorded measurements on an oscilloscope every two minutes. The SPARS had their own barracks there, too.

Because it was wartime, the SPARS kept a gun in the LORAN room. They practiced in a pistol range set up in the basement of a building in Chatham, with some of them achieving high marksman status.[71] A well-known photograph shows a laughing Freeman, in uniform, aiming two pistols in her right hand and one in her left at the photographer.

Freeman loved Chatham; she also loved a local man named Sullie Eldridge, whom she married in February 1946. After the war, the pair made their home in Chatham and raised a family here.

"HYACINTHS TO MY SOUL"

In her newsletter, Mrs. Matteson took particular pride in the contributions women in uniforms made to the war effort. In January 1943, she writes, "The women have the lead this month with Pearl Nickerson teaching under her maiden name as code instructor to 800 men at the Radio Institute of the YMCA Trade and Technical School in NY."

Back at home, "Marjorie Hammond has mumps on both sides of her face—Kenneth Pratt fell on the Mayflower Shop steps and broke his right leg." And newlywed Harold Dunbar was in Cape Cod Hospital.

In February, the army took over the Acme Laundry to launder the clothing of the growing numbers of military personnel. This was a winter in which snow had covered the ground continuously since Christmas. "Whooping cough and grippe have superseded mumps of last month, adults are having mumps this winter."

New air raid horns were installed at Bearse's and Roy Meservey's garages. Two more would be installed to complete the system. The Warning Center was in Matteson's own home, and she was on duty twenty-four hours a day.

"We are all working and knitting and keeping our chins up for you," she concluded her March 1943 letter. "Bless everyone of you."

Staff Sergeant John H. Nickerson, who grew up on Main Street, in his World War II uniform. Nickerson attended South Plains Army Flying School in Lubbock, Texas, and served as a glider pilot in Europe. After the war, he returned home to run several businesses and raise a family with his wife, Jane. *Photo courtesy of Ginny Nickerson.*

In April, she observes, "The town is very quiet and the men feel it when they come home for a few days." The summer of 1943 was looking like it would be a true wartime summer, with many of the hotels closed. "Chatham Bars Garage is the Coast Guard Commissary now, and the chauffeurs' quarters houses the Red Cross Servicemen's Club." Those hotels that stayed open collected their guests' food ration stamps so that the hotel chef could purchase food.[72]

Scotty Brown's mother received Scotty's Purple Heart, awarded posthumously. "You are all writing me swell letters—they are hyacinths to my soul, keep it up," Matteson wrote. "I love receiving them and I have them all saved in a file."

It was still snowing and cold.

At some point in 1943, Congregational Church officials asked Alice Stallknecht to remove her murals from the church. The agreement had been that they were on loan and could be removed upon request. The true story behind the removal of the murals is yet to be told. Church records of the time provide no narrative, only a confusing account of a vote or of more than one vote.

Alice's son Fred, who was serving as a lieutenant commander in the United States Naval Reserves and was stationed abroad at the time, later wrote, "There were many changes in the church, either in policy, or in the succession of ministers."[73] He continued, "I was in Europe, in the War, when the paintings came out, and have no evidence to offer, except that it was a painful rejection for the painter."

Time magazine was blunt: "Upset at seeing itself mirrored in its own house of worship, the congregation voted to return the pictures to the artist."[74]

In May 1943, "Bob Hardy has been promoted to Captain, is flying cargo from Memphis," Matteson reports. Hardy, whose great-grandfather Josiah Hardy kept the Chatham Light from 1872 to 1897, was a graduate of the Dallas Aviation School in Texas. After Hardy graduated from Chatham High in 1937 in a class of twelve, his mother "mortgaged the house and sent me to flying school. Flying always intrigued me." Hardy was hired by American Airlines in 1940. When World War II began, the civilian pilots at American Airlines continued flying at home.[75]

On May 6, Arthur W. Edwards, age eighty-six, died at his daughter's house in Wollaston. Since the '20s, Edwards had been famous as the man everyone believed was the model for Joseph Lincoln's character in his novel *Shavings* and in the long-running Broadway play adapted from the book. When he died, the *New York Times* called Edwards's shop "the scene of most of the action in the book."[76] Edwards left behind a widow, Mertis, two daughters and a son. He was buried in East Harwich.

EAT ALL THE MEAT YOU CAN GET

In June 1943 it was hot—eighty degrees in the sun. The start of the summer brought a little entertainment to lives that had become drab under wartime rationing and precautions. "We had a fine carnival the day after Memorial Day, around 800 people from the town got out, saw Harold Tuttle and a goat act the clown, bought hot dogs, coke, peanuts and ice cream," Matteson wrote. The Coast Guard and the army played a baseball game.

"Meat is scarce, it goes to all you servicemen, God bless you, eat all you can get, and we will all think of you as we count our points and eat what we can get." But this being Chatham, plenty of mackerel and striped bass were waiting to be caught on North Beach.

"Neither lowered gasoline rations nor crowded trains appear to quench this annual urge to take off for some place," a *New York Times* travel writer expounded on June 6. How to get to Chatham with little gas? In Grand Central Station, board the Cape Codder or the Neptune, of course. On June 18, the train would make daily runs to Hyannis, where a bus connection would bring visitors to Chatham.

Harry Cutts recalled that gasoline rationing complicated the trip from Brookline to Chatham. He and his mother would take the train from Boston to Hyannis. There they would catch a red New England Transportation bus to Chatham. Finally, an Eldredge taxi at the Tydol Station on Main Street would convey them to their house on Champlain Road.[77]

In July, the servicemen and civilians had a tug of war. The civilians won. The hotels were filled, but not many houses were rented. In Chatham's version of Rosie the Riveter, "Edith Curtiss is driving the delivery truck for Roy; first girl in town and she does a swell job." In August, local girl Gladys Goodspeed married Dick Lumpkin, the navy man from Baltimore who was working at Chatham Station C. This was one of many wartime marriages that would bring new blood to town.

In September, the War Fund drive was "over the top." It has been a "very busy profitable summer. The Inns which were open, homes, restaurants and business are very satisfied with the season. It's been like old times, having the town full…And have the fishermen been making money, too, I'll say so," Matteson gushed.

Although beach plums and grapes were scarce, housewives were canning vegetables "to the limit" to get through the winter. Oyster season opened, but "short of help, the home war cry." In fact, Oscar Doane maintained the

Wartime at Home

"Short of help, the home war cry," wrote Edna Matteson in her World War II newsletter. During the war, Chatham's fish and seafood were abundant as ever—if the manpower was available to get it. *Photo courtesy of the Chatham, Massachusetts Historical Society.*

town's highways "practically alone," and Charlie Peltier was the only one left to deliver ice.

On October 9, Augustus Bearse turned ninety and received the gold-topped Post Cane from Selectman Edwin Eldridge. The cane had been given to Chatham's oldest male citizen since 1901. "I have had to have a doctor only twice," Bearse boasted. "Once for typhoid fever when I was 14, and a few years ago when I was afflicted with shingles."[78] At ninety, Bearse attended the Congregational church regularly.

When Italy surrendered, Edwin Eldredge rang the Methodist church bell. "Sirens blew for ½ hour and rockets, cannons and pistols, and cars blowing as they traveled through town completed the uproar."

On October 10, 1943, thirty-four-year-old Virginia Avis Harding married Arthur James Durkee Jr., an older man with a grown daughter and a grandchild. This was Durkee's third marriage—his second wife, Mary, had died at age thirty-six in April 1942. Arthur moved to Prospect House, Virginia's childhood home, which the newlyweds shared with Edith, Virginia's mother. Down Main Street, Durkee opened a meat and vegetable store in the old Tuttle's Market.

The town topped $86,000 in war bonds purchased. The army said it would place a plaque in a bomber stating that the bomber was made possible by the people of Chatham in memory of Robert Scott Brown.

CLAM CHOWDER AND MARYLAND FRIED CHICKEN

While about three hundred of Chatham's men and women would leave town to join the war effort, just as many outsiders came to town.

Henry Schalizki grew up in Baltimore in a family with a tradition of working on the Baltimore and Ohio (B&O) Railroad. One grandfather did hard manual work in a boiler room while his father, Harry, worked as a B&O clerk.

Young Henry used to scrub the marble stoops of Baltimore's row houses at the rate of ten cents a stoop, working until he had collected enough change to catch the trolley to the movies and pay for a candy bar as well. After he graduated from Baltimore City College High School in 1938, Henry worked first with Montgomery Ward, filling orders in the warehouse on roller skates, and then went into the family business, the B&O. But "it didn't click with me," he said, and in April 1942, four months after the invasion of Pearl Harbor, he enlisted in the U.S. Navy. Because he was only twenty, his mother signed a consent form.[79]

He spent about a year and a half working in the Navy Department building in Washington, D.C., and in November 1943, he received orders to report to Chatham. "Mother said, 'Where's Chatham?'" he recalled. They consulted a map.

He caught the old Cape Codder train—New York to Hyannis—and then a bus to Chatham in the evening. When he arrived at the four-story Hawthorne Hotel on Shore Road, "they said 'What are you doing here?' I said 'I don't know.'" He was assigned to a windowless room at the top of a flight of stairs with three other men—Wes Ewald, Jesse Wickham, Earl Viets—and a sink. A married sailor who had moved into lodgings with his wife had just vacated the bunk assigned to Schalizki. "They didn't have any fresh sheets and I wasn't going to sleep on those sheets, so I tore the whole bed apart and slept on the mattress," Schalizki recalled.

Chief Bradford came to see Schalizki in the morning and told him he was going to work as a Teletype operator under tight wartime security at Chatham Station C. His new boss would be Dick Lumpkin. Coincidentally, the pair had both graduated from the same high school in 1938—Lumpkin in February and Schalizki in June—but they did not meet until the war threw them together in Chatham.

Every day, a bus picked up the navy men at the Hawthorne and drove them to the radio station in Chatham Port for round-the-clock watches that began at 8:00 a.m., 4:00 p.m. and midnight. (The navy women, WAVES,

Henry Schalizki (seated) was reunited with his former boss, Dick Lumpkin, for the first time in nearly sixty-five years in May 2008. The two men, both from Baltimore, worked closely at Chatham Station C as teletypewriters during World War II. *Photo by the author.*

who would arrive in June 1944, lived in a now-demolished inn called Rose Acres off Cross Street.)[80] After Schalizki acquired a bicycle from an inebriated cook, he often cycled to work from the Hawthorne.

As civilian guards patrolled the perimeter and entrances to the thirteen-acre wireless radio station campus, Schalizki worked in the operations building, a red brick building on Orleans Road. During the war, trees obscured the buildings that the Marconi Corporation erected in 1914. The large room accommodated about thirty radio intercept operators. Dick Lumpkin supervised the three Teletype shifts—three people per shift—in the small rear room. When the lights were off in the building, it was absolutely black.

The bulk of the personnel at the station were listeners; by 1943, sixty radio operators had been assigned to each shift, around the clock. The German submarine service had an Achilles heel: Admiral Karl Dönitz, commander of the German *Kriegsmarine*, insisted that he maintain regular radio contact with his U-boats.[81] Messages encoded through the Enigma cipher machine were sent from Berlin to the U-boats, where they were decoded. The U-boats then responded in turn to the messages, giving vital information about their supplies of fuel and torpedoes. Dönitz did not believe that the British were capable of breaking the Enigma code, but they had done exactly that through their work at Bletchley Park.

The navy's radio network extended from Greenland to Recife, Brazil, and included five stations in the United States and one in Puerto Rico.[82] Station C had two goals: intercepting messages sent to Berlin from the U-boats and pinpointing their locations.[83] A ten-megahertz rhombic antenna at the station was pointed toward Berlin.[84] Listeners inside the station turned dials on their radio sets to listen through the wavelengths in the band they were monitoring. When they heard a "beep," they would stop and pick up the message, which was in encoded German and relayed through Morse code. The radio listener would record the message and transcribe it for a Teletype operator, who would then send the message to the naval annex in Arlington, Virginia. There, a staff using linked Enigma machines called "bombes" began the arduous process of first decoding and then translating the message from German.

Usually, within the first two or three letters of an arriving code group, sister stations on the intercept network as far south as Recife, Brazil, would be alerted to make a direction reading. This, together with a similar radio compass reading from Chatham, was used to triangulate the U-boat's position.[85]

"The type work was exciting, the secrecy was exciting," Schalizki recalled many years later. "We were followed by security people all the time. I didn't even tell my closest friends what I was doing." After the war, the 317 men and women assigned to the Chatham station during World War II signed secrecy agreements that were rescinded only about a decade later.

During the war, probably no single person at the station completely understood the work the station did.[86] Just how vital Chatham's work in transmitting U-boat intelligence was became apparent as the numbers of American ships sunk radically declined during 1943.

Every twelve days, the navy men had three days off. "I was told: If you're not a Nickerson, Eldredge or Bearse you don't belong up here," Schalizki remembered. But this was wartime, and most people loved sailors. Schalizki made good friends and often went to Hardings Beach with his roommates and townspeople. He organized daytime clambakes on the beach, taking care to douse the fires well before dark due to blackout regulations. Schalizki's wartime photo album highlights trips from Plymouth to Provincetown.

He also grew close to the Kilhefner family. Raymond Kilhefner was also an outsider in town, having come from a family of farmers in Lancaster,

Pennsylvania. He married a local girl, Agnes Doane, known as "Altie," who grew up on Old Harbor Road and whose father was a fisherman. Initially, Kilhefner worked as a mechanic in a garage, but when Schalizki knew him, he owned one or more gas stations. Kilhefner was also a Mason, which created an additional bond with Schalizki, whose grandfather was a Mason.

Agnes Kilhefner was about four years younger than Henry and grew up on Cross Street a few doors down from Dr. Minnie Buck. During the war, she was a student at Pembroke College, then the women's division of Brown University, in Providence.

A photograph shows Schalizki, in uniform, sitting on what is probably the back stoop of the Kilhefner house. Next to him is Mrs. Kilhefner. The short sleeves of the women's cotton dresses suggest a warm day. In Schalizki's lap is a colander of strawberries—this must be June 1943 or 1944. Perhaps it was even June 25, Agnes's nineteenth or twentieth birthday. And perhaps that was the evening Schalizki introduced the Kilhefners to Maryland fried chicken, which he prepared in their kitchen. Schalizki himself was learning the Chatham culinary lingo: "cabinets" were milkshakes with ice cream, and

In Chatham, navy teletypewriter Henry Schalizki learned to make quahog chowder while introducing friends Raymond and Altie Kilhefner of Cross Street to Maryland fried chicken. *Photo courtesy of Henry Schalizki.*

"tonics" were Coca-Colas. And, of course, Schalizki learned what a quahog was and how to make a good Cape Cod clam chowder.

On Main Street, "the sailors' hangout" was the New Yorker Bar and Grill, now the Chatham Squire. The Teletype operators who worked the four-to-midnight shift would often go to the New Yorker for lobster rolls and beers before walking back to the Hawthorne on Shore Road. Another popular spot was Jacob's Garden on the corner of Skyline Drive and Old Queen Anne Road. The beer hall that overlooked Lover's Lake eventually burned down during a spectacular fire in the 1950s.

The USO sponsored dances and performances in its club on Chatham Bars Avenue. "You should see the old chauffeur's quarters, remodeled into the new USO club," Matteson wrote. The club had a lounge, a big fireplace, books, a game room, a kitchen "and a room upstairs with two beds, for day rest."

"Generally it was pretty quiet here, everything was dark," Lumpkin said. It was so dark that "you could walk into a fire hydrant without seeing it."

While Schalizki and Lumpkin toiled in secrecy at the radio station, townspeople continued to collect warm clothing—402 pounds by December.

Death and Birth and More Death

Chatham suffered its second casualty when Marine Robert E. Buck died on February 22, 1944, in action en route to the Marshall Islands.

Two days later, triplets were born to Susie and Clarence Frank, "three boys, two living," Matteson notes. The boys, who were born at Cape Cod Hospital, were named Jeffrey Carlton and Jerry Clinton.

A few days after their birth, Susie, who worked as a secretary at the Acme Laundry, brought her twin boys home to West Chatham. While Susie was one of Chatham's Eldridges, her husband, Clarence, was a commercial fisherman from Nova Scotia whom she met in Boston.

Matteson concluded that month's newsletter: "The town looks just the same, the fishermen have been doing well, and next month I will know how the bowling season has stacked up."

On March 10, Joseph Lincoln died of a heart attack in his apartment at the Virginia Inn in Winter Park, Florida. He was seventy-four. He left behind his widow, Florence, his son, Major Joseph Freeman Lincoln of Philadelphia and Washington, D.C., now overseas with the intelligence department, and two granddaughters. His ashes were sent back to Chatham for burial at Union Cemetery.

"As a boy he roamed the Cape, fishing, riding in the old stagecoach from Hyannis to Chatham, and learning much of the lives and thoughts and humble aspirations of lightkeepers, fishermen, life savers and the cracker-barrel oracles who abounded in every village store," the *New York Times* eulogized on March 11, 1944.

Lincoln's final novel, *The Bradshaws of Harniss*, was published just three months before his death. In it, he "makes a concession to time only in telling of Zenas Bradshaw's nephew winning the Distinguished Flying Cross and the efforts of small businessmen to keep themselves going."[87]

In April, the *New York Times* reported that Lincoln had left an estate of $200,000, a considerable sum in 1944.

In May, Matteson's chronicle to the troops was interrupted as she caught pneumonia and lay in bed for six weeks. When she returned to her typewriter, she was full of news. L.V. Eldredge caught a three-pound salmon at Goose Pond, "and they got plenty of trout, too." To date, Chatham had contributed $456,225 to all war drives. About 250 of the town's sons and daughters had entered into the armed services or war work at home, and all were receiving Matteson's newsletter.[88]

In June, despite her illness and the war dragging on, Matteson's tone is chipper. "It looks like a good, busy summer," she writes. Fifteen graduated from Chatham High, and "Mrs. Joseph Lincoln christened a new ship, the *Joseph C. Lincoln*."

"JUST A WANDERING MEAT CUTTER"

Sometimes a major emotional trauma can be wrapped up in small things: a radio-phonograph, a little hand-held vacuum cleaner, a cedar chest, a car radio, an engagement ring and a life insurance policy.

Such was the case with the 1943 wartime marriage of Virginia Harding and Arthur Durkee. With the benefit of hindsight, it would seem that certain events conspired to destroy their marriage. Living in a household under the thumb of Edith, Virginia's mother, must have been hard on all three. But wartime housing was short, and Edith would otherwise live alone. In reading the Harding family papers, one has an image of Virginia as a pampered young woman whose father was devoted to her. Heman's sudden death in 1936 left the two women stranded at home together. Arthur Durkee was different from the staid, reliable Heman, and his introduction to the household must have created a shock. At some point, probably during the

Alice Stallknecht's painting of Virginia Harding is one of the few that flattered its subject. Harding, like her father, Heman, was a major player in town politics and the Eldredge Public Library for over four decades. *Photo by the author from a painting at the Chatham, Massachusetts Historical Society.*

summer of 1944, Durkee moved out of the Harding family home, leaving Virginia alone with her mother—and humiliated.

At the end of September, Virginia typed a letter to Durkee in which she alternately threatened him, insulted him and pleaded with him to return. "Up to the time I married you, you were just a wandering meat cutter," she types in words that almost burn off the page decades later. (Virginia, using her training as her father's legal secretary, slipped carbon paper behind the letter; many years later, she donated the carbon copy, along with her father's legal files, to the Chatham Historical Society. Interestingly, the carbon has been annotated in pencil, as though Virginia spent time rereading it after she presumably mailed the original to Durkee.)

Virginia resented the success of the grocery store, which she felt she had toiled to build up as much as Durkee had. "You haven't helped your business any by this little 'go-round,'" she writes, "for there are some who say they will never trade with you because you have treated a good wife so shamefully. A wife-deserter gets short shrift in a small town.

"I don't hate you, yet, but I'm gosh-awful mad with you, as I have a right to be," she adds. She says that if Durkee doesn't return to her, she's going to "provide entertainment" to the town by making public the details of their estrangement. "You were crazy enough about me to marry me, so I guess you'd better be crazy enough about me to live with me, to love me and support me in the style to which I am entitled." She calls marriage "sacred" and says she doesn't want to be separated from Durkee. She doesn't believe in divorce.

And by the way, she adds, what about those things he promised her? What about that hand-held vacuum cleaner?

Yet just after New Year's Day, Virginia, now receiving her mail at the Wayside Inn down Main Street from her family home, is planning to seek an uncontested divorce and waive alimony. ("I'm not grabby because there hasn't been anything for me to grab," she had written to Durkee.) The divorce trial will be shorter and simpler "and without all of the embarrassment that would accompany a contested case," Virginia's attorney, Harold Williams, wrote her on January 19. In stark contrast to Virginia's earlier threats of letting the entire town know of her unhappy situation, Williams assured her that he would try to have the case heard "when no one will be present." Virginia and Durkee's divorce would be made final during the summer of 1945.

At this same time, Virginia was beginning her reign in the Eldredge Public Library. Her father, Heman, served for forty years as the library's president and treasurer. Upon his death in 1936, Virginia took on those roles.

The trouble was, Virginia was not her father, and from almost the beginning she made trouble for Edna May Hardy, who had served as librarian since 1911. Edna May had gone deaf in her twenties,[89] and instead of assisting Edna, Virginia contrived to make Edna's life a living hell. By 1940, Virginia had removed Edna from the book purchasing committee, and shortly after that, Virginia required that Edna and the library's custodian pick up their quarterly paychecks in person, at her house. If Edna was sick or on vacation, Virginia took over the job—authorizing pay for herself. Virginia "considered the Library a kind of Harding Family enterprise, not a community resource."[90] This tense situation continued until the early 1950s; Edna retired in 1954 and died thirteen years later.

Now Enter the Royals

"What with WAVES, SPARS, Navy, Coast Guard, jeeps, Commissary trucks, the town was busy, now it is packed to the limit with summer folks and the streets down town are crowded every day, all day," Matteson wrote in July 1944. Joseph Lincoln would be missed around town.

It may have been during her summer visit to Chatham in 1944 that Crown Princess Juliana of the Netherlands summoned Doc Keene over to attend one of her three little daughters in a cottage at Chatham Bars Inn. In May 1940, as the German army invaded the Netherlands, the royal family had fled Holland to live in exile in London, where Prince Bernhard joined the Royal Air Force. But in June 1940, the princess and her two young daughters, Beatrix and Irene, traveled by ship to Canada, moving into a house in Ottawa. The princess's third daughter, Margriet, was born there in January 1943.

Outside the princess's quarters, the FBI stopped Doc Keene for questioning, Doc Keene reminisced many years later.[91] When he was asked for his credentials, Doc Keene said they were in his black bag. The FBI agent continued to question the doctor on the doorstep until the princess intervened and asked him in to examine the sick child.

A charming photo in the *New York Times* on September 1, 1944, shows Princess Juliana walking hand in hand on Shore Road with her three blond daughters, all wearing white dresses and white shoes. "Netherlands Royalty Awaiting Country's Liberation," reads the headline.

In 1948, Princess Juliana would ascend to the Dutch throne, with Beatrix following her in 1980.

"We have had only a few days of fog—when the old Stone Horse wailed for us, so everyone has been able to get to the beach and sun and picnic," Matteson wrote, referring to the lightship anchored off Chatham. Margaret Guild, Alice Guild's daughter, in the Army Nurse Corps, was now a first lieutenant. Hilda Eldredge, who had joined the army in June 1943, advanced to sergeant at Camp Butner in North Carolina.

BLOW, WIND, BLOW

On the night of September 14, 1944, winds up to 100 miles an hour whipped through Chatham, scooping boats out of the water and tossing them into newly formed pools. At 1:20 a.m., a gust of 105 miles an hour was recorded in a rain that was a "blinding deluge."[92] The gale threw the steeple of the First Universalist Church to the ground; telephone poles swayed at forty-five-degree angles. The wind buckled the Village Hall in South Chatham.

"No lives lost, and one house destroyed," Matteson wrote. "But what a mess around the shore!"

Wartime at Home

While Chatham managed to escape the destruction of the legendary Hurricane of '38, the wreckage left by the Hurricane of '44 is clearly visible at Stage Harbor. *Photo courtesy of the Chatham, Massachusetts Historical Society.*

A tidal wave washed up from Stage Harbor across the yard of the house where Alice Stallknecht and her husband, Carol Wight, lived. "The wind was like the teeth of a rake," Wight said later.[93]

Boats washed up Stage Harbor three hundred yards into the marsh. The tin building in Kenney's boatyard on Stage Harbor Road collapsed. The Freezer Wharf was gone. The fishermen said the tidal wave was eleven feet above the ten-foot tide. The Sea Scouts, directed by Dessie Eldredge, have "done a great job helping clear up at Kenney's boat yard."

Eighteen-year-old Reggie Nickerson was clearing up the area by Alice Stallknecht's house when Stallknecht spotted him.[94] Stallknecht was then embarking on yet a third ambitious mural, *Every Man to His Trade*. Stallknecht asked Reggie and scout Ed Proudfoot to pose for her, which they did. This mural, too, takes Christ as its centerpiece—Christ the carpenter. Slim Hutchings, now older, perhaps stockier, again posed as Christ.

The mural spans the life cycle, with Alice's young grandson, George, shown in a cradle, flanked by his mother and father, in a square in the upper left. In the lower right, Florence Harding clasps her hands in a cemetery. And in thirty separate panels, Stallknecht depicts the comedy and tragedy of life. Doc Keene stands in a group of people at a fair outside the Methodist church, pointing to a cake that he wants. Spencer Loveland is shown hunting on Monomoy, while George Cahoon is weir fishing. Four stranded Nova Scotia fishermen stand outside the town hall, hats in hand, thanking a small figure in the doorway for providing them with food and tickets back to Nova Scotia. Alice's husband, Carol, is posed in front of the monument to Champlain's arrival, which he helped to erect across from the family house.

Because Stallknecht's murals had by now been removed from the Congregational church, Stallknecht bought a railroad freight station that came up for auction and installed the three murals inside it in her yard. For many years, the public was invited to tour the murals just outside Stallknecht's house in her "Studio in the Field." In their new location, the murals continued to be advertised in guidebooks to the town.[95]

During the hurricane, the Wights' barn lost its roof, and Alice's freight station gallery was badly wrecked, "but I jacked it up and it's all right today," Wight later said.[96] Also, during the storm a strange assortment of objects, including a typewriter, a chair and a life preserver from a torpedoed London steamer, washed up in the yard. Wight stowed them on a shelf in his shed along with fragments from a Native American skull that someone found on the property.

Recovery from the hurricane was slow, and in October the Mitchell River Bridge was still closed. "Work is going on all over the Cape, patching roofs, shingling, cutting up fallen trees, etc.," Matteson wrote.

A month later, "another blow and sort of tidal wave," she wrote. The Victory Market closed after two and a half years; Reggie Nickerson was now stationed at Keesler Field. "Election Day didn't seem the same without Dr. Worthing and his sidewalk discussions." Elizabeth Reynard, a Chatham summer resident and the author of *The Narrow Land: Folk Chronicles of Old Cape Cod*, was promoted to lieutenant commander in the WAVES. Reynard would be the second highest–ranking officer in the WAVES and would also have the distinction of designing the group's uniform.

Thanksgiving Day that year was marred by the death of another of Chatham's native sons, Staff Sergeant Roland Wallace James. James, who had graduated from Chatham High in the class of 1935 with Scotty Brown, was killed in Metz, France.

The holidays were quiet. "The wind just blows all the time now, as you all very well know," Matteson writes. It was cold, and the first snow fell. A number of local women joined the WAVES. "I feel that [you] are all my children, whether you are young or old, and I am interested in each one, what you are doing, and how you are making out."

At the town meeting in February 1945, a vote of 222 to 0 allocated $35,000 for a fish packing plant with a stall house to accommodate 20 fishermen, a bulkhead and unloading frontage. This would replace a row of fishing shacks overlooking Aunt Lydia's Cove.[97]

A RED CAP, A BOMB AND SOME GOOD NEWS

By March, a reader can sense Mrs. Matteson's weariness both with the war and with the winter. "Harry Daughaday seems rather feeble this spring, I think, but he still has his red cap pulled down around his ears."

The town was still seething about the government's seizure of Monomoy by eminent domain in 1944. Fifteen state senators, representatives and "bird authorities from all over the Cape" held a hearing on the federal government's taking of Monomoy. Selectman Edwin Eldredge acted as moderator, "and he told them some things they didn't know." The matter was remanded to Washington, D.C., for further consideration. On March 4, the town upped the ante by filing a $1 million damage suit against the federal government "as the climax of a four-year fight to prevent the taking of 3,000 acres of land for another bird refuge."[98]

During the war, the military had been using Monomoy as a bombing range. In the spring of 1945, the navy was particularly interested in developing thousand-pound guided bombs.[99] The challenge lay in steering the bomb from an airplane to an aircraft carrier moving at full speed.

To work on the problem the navy called in Edwin Land, who had founded Polaroid in 1937. Land's idea was to attach a compact movie camera in the nose of the bomb and then, later, study the movie of the bomb as it fell.

Land and his assistant, William McCune, drove one evening from Boston to Chatham, arriving late. They found all of the inns closed, but the lights were on in the lobby of one—probably the Wayside. The innkeeper never did appear, but the pair occupied themselves all night playing puzzles in the lobby.

The next day, Land went out to the bombing range on Monomoy, a spot his physicist, David Gray, dubbed "just a sand bar dropped by ocean currents." While Land moved along on the bomb tests, the war abruptly ended.[100] "The Cape looks shabby," Matteson wrote in April.

So many of the trees standing are almost or really dead, the foliage is very slow in coming out...Almost all houses have been either repaired,

Edwin Land, the founder of Polaroid, came to Chatham to study bombs at Monomoy. Arriving late, he and his assistant found all of the inns closed, but the lighted lobby in one—probably the Wayside—beckoned. They sat up all night playing puzzles no doubt set out to entertain servicemen and women. *Photo by the author.*

patched up, and the broken tree stumps and dead wood with no one to remove them makes the Cape look badly. The Government has said the Cape is truly a fire hazard.

Yet the war news was improving. Kenneth Nickerson, reported missing, was released from a German POW camp. Walter Hopkins, hospitalized for frozen feet, "can now hike six miles." And Harry Daughaday "has at last shed his red plaid cap—He wishes it was summer." Of the $5,000 needed to repair the Universal church's steeple, damaged in the hurricane of the previous September, $1,000 had been raised.

And on April 30, Hitler committed suicide in his bunker.

"I am writing this as the President reads the proclamation for the cessation of hostilities in Europe," Matteson wrote. "The sirens have blown, the churches are holding services, all the stores are closed, and I say 'Thank God.'"

By May, life was perking up. "It seems from the talk around, that the hotels and rooming houses plan to do very well this summer," she noted. "Many summer house owners are down early this year."

Early in the month, when the papers were signed marking the official surrender of Germany, Schalizki remembered German admiral Karl Dönitz ordering the U-boats to surface. "They popped up like popcorn," he said.

And then "it was over so quick," Schalizki said. "Suddenly everyone was gone." Overnight, Schalizki found himself on a tanker headed to Oahu, where he would spend the next nine months. There had been no time for goodbyes or for exchanging addresses.[101]

Rumors abounded that RCA would soon take over the radio station again. "John Emery is able to sit out part of the day under the trees on the lawn," Edna Matteson noted.

After nearly three years, Matteson ended her newsletters. "We have had fog and then more fog, not so good for the fishermen, but it has cleared up through the day, so the summer people have had really hot days for the beach parties…I will be writing you all again before long."

Alice Guild and her grandson Gene walk back from a swim at Oyster Pond, 1943. During the war, tar washing up on the beaches from burning tankers off the coast caused many to scrub their feet in lighter fluid after a swim. *Photo courtesy of Gene Guild.*

VICTORY AT LAST

At 7:00 p.m. on Tuesday, August 14, an announcement came over the radio that the war had ended. During the previous week, atomic bombs dropped over Hiroshima and Nagasaki had finally ended the conflict. Summer resident Elinor Miller recalls sitting in the dining room of the Mattaquasson Hotel with her parents when the war's end was announced on the radio. "Since gas rationing ended literally the moment the war was over," Miller's father departed immediately on the Hyannis train to pick up the family car in New York.[102]

People poured out their pent-up feelings and worries of three years and eight months. It seemed that no one wanted to be home alone that evening.

"The screeching of fire and air raid sirens, the continuous blowing of horns, large gatherings of people in the streets and fire trucks being driven around with crowds of people on them featured Chatham's celebration of the end of hostilities with Japan," the *Cape Cod Times* reported on August 15.

Newly divorced Virginia Harding nursed private woes that evening. "I pinch-hit for the Police Department, standing by on the radio and telephone," she wrote to her attorney, Harold Williams, about a month later. "And did it burn me up to have to sign the Radio Log 'V. Durkee.'" Virginia wanted her own name, Harding, back.[103]

The USO mobile unit provided music for dancing in the block near the Mayflower Shop. Chatham's four churches, too, were filled to capacity.[104] The town had "tamed down" by 11:00 p.m., and "no accidents or fires were reported, although a few slightly inebriated individuals could be seen."

A couple of days later, Flotilla 602 of the Coast Guard Auxiliary celebrated the end of the war with a "strictly stag" clambake at Eastward, Ho! Country Club. In the morning, about sixty men played golf and horseshoes, at 2:30 p.m. they sat down to a clambake and they finished the day with boat races and a tug of war.[105]

The weekend of August 17 represented the first weekend with gas enough for all. "The release of gasoline from rationing brought out just about every car still in existence, from the latest thing to come off the assembly lines in 1942 to old timers that were new in 1924, or just after WWI," the Cape's police observed.[106]

Summer resident Harry Cutts remembers that after the war "we would load up my parents' '37 Packard and three hours later, from Brookline, would arrive in Chatham."

Less than a week after the war's end, headlines were declaring "Record Building Boom Seen for Cape Cod." It was just a matter of collecting the men and the materials for it to take off, said one architect.

"It was almost a new world here after the war," Samuel S. Rogers later recalled. "I can't remember too many new summer people coming here when we were small. After the war it changed. All the developments began."[107]

As a character in one of Phoebe Atwood Taylor's Cape Cod mysteries proclaims:

> *Whenever I thought about peace, during the war, I forgot all the things that went along with it. You know, like tourists, and strikes, and sky-high prices, and the roads so packed you hardly dare drive on 'em, and crazy outlanders speeding around curves, and throwing beer bottles and paper plates all over.*[108]

On August 25, it was raining heavily when Mrs. Joseph Lincoln, Florence to her friends, went outside her Shore Road house to investigate why she was hearing the horn of her car blowing repeatedly. Smoke billowed from the garage doors and its roof. Firefighters found the car blazing, a total wreck. Damage from the fire was $2,500.

Three days later, Virginia Harding, as the paper now referred to her, gave a talk at the Chatham Historical Society on Chatham's seven old mills. "People should be more careful of old things, as this is the only source for record," she told gathered society members.[109]

One night at about this time, someone coaxed a cow into the Main Street School. "It has smashed up all the desks," someone remembered.[110]

THIS AND THAT

If the taking of Monomoy wasn't enough, now the state planning board had its eye on Hardings Beach, "Chatham's most important beach," as a resolution at town meeting called it. The resolution asked the state planners to develop new beaches rather than seizing "an accessible, developed beach from a small town to which this beach means so much."

On June 1, 1946, the new fish pier was ready for use. Electric hoist buckets could lift twelve hundred pounds of fish, and a full load could be raised up from a boat at low tide in forty-five seconds. That summer, "the Fish Pier was a constant point of interest to our Summer Visitors as well as a large number of natives and many compliments were expressed as to the neat and efficient way the fish were handled," the 1946 *Report of the Town Officers* boasted. The pier, two buildings and a parking area cost about $54,000. The project was called "the greatest added single investment the town has ever made."

On June 1, 1946, the town's new fish pier opened. Electric hoist buckets could lift a full load of fish from a boat at low tide in forty-five seconds. The pier quickly became a new tourist attraction. *Photo courtesy of William and Nancy Koerner.*

The fish pier also had "an old wood stove" where, "during cold, stormy winter nights," the Coast Guard and the fishermen kept vigil together "watching the boats straining on their moorings in the harbor."[111]

On June 27, a victory party was held at Chatham Bars Inn. Each veteran was presented with a silver medal and certificates framed by local photographer Richard Kelsey. About three hundred of Chatham's men and women had served in the war, and their names would soon be listed on an honor roll plaque that hangs to this day in what is now the Community Building—the old Main Street School. Chatham's Veterans of Foreign Wars Post 8607 was later renamed the Brown-James-Buck Post to honor the memory of three men who did not return: Robert Scott Brown, Roland Wallace James and Robert Buck.

EDWARD ROWE SNOW'S WEIRD WALK

In May 1945, the forty-three-year-old nautical writer Edward Rowe Snow, on a seven-week hiking trip across Cape Cod, came to town. Snow's main obsession was shipwrecks. Having hiked to Chatham from Orleans via Nauset Beach, swimming the last stretch, Snow checked into the Wayside Inn and lay in bed during his first night reading the first volume of William C. Smith's *History of Chatham, Mass.*[112] The next morning, walking up Main

Street toward the ocean, he spotted, apparently at random, a quarter board from the ship *Lamartine*. When he rang the bell at the Harding house, Virginia answered the door and invited him into the living room to chat with her mother, Edith. Later, Virginia drove Snow to the Atwood House Museum and let him in through a side door with her key.

"It was cold and had an unlived-in feeling, but there was much inside to interest me," Snow remarked. Just as the travel writer Eleanor Early had been a decade earlier, Snow was drawn to the "hair wreath" woven from the hair of Rebecca Atkins and her eleven children.[113]

But Snow was after light keeper Josiah Hardy's journal, and Virginia decided to drive him to the home of Hardy's granddaughter Edna, the Eldredge Library's deaf librarian whom Virginia had been tormenting for a decade now. Edna graciously turned the journal over to Snow for his inspection.

On later days of his visit, Snow saw Alice Stallknecht's "truly inspiring" murals and declared himself "deeply moved."[114] He also spent time with "Good Walter" Eldredge—a man noted for building a two-story house right on the beach using the wood he gathered from seventeen separate shipwrecks.

In June, voters at a special town meeting were asked to expend $10,000 to erect a war veterans' memorial. They were also asked to execute a lease with the owners of Great Hill, which had been occupied by the radar camp. The town wanted to maintain a building there for emergency veterans' housing. Under the Lanham Act of September 8, 1939, towns had to provide such housing. Ten units were needed in Chatham. Eventually, eleven veterans and their families were housed in five converted Army Air Forces buildings on Great Hill.

In November, Chatham Station C was well on its way to returning to civilian status. In addition, ground was broken in South Chatham for a new RCA transmitter building. On Forest Beach Road, three and a half miles from the receiving station in Chatham Port, the station would consist of two buildings with three 350-foot towers. One building would house the equipment and the office; the other would house the station's operator.[115] Chatham would be the first station to receive word when the *Andrea Doria* and the *Stockholm* collided in July 1956 in fog off Nantucket.[116]

I SLEEP BETTER IN THE SEA AIR

In 1947, members of the Congregational Church voted "that the clerk write to five men admitted to our church during World War I to see if they wish to retain their membership," according to a history of the church. "They

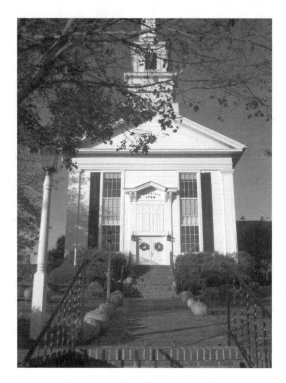

During the war, in a move that remains shrouded in mystery, church officials voted to ask Alice Stallknecht to remove her murals *Christ Preaching to the Multitude* and *The Circle Supper*. It was a blow to the artist. *Photo by the author.*

had not been heard from since 1930." That same year, church attendance fluctuated between twelve and forty-five, with membership rising to between seventy-two and one hundred in the summer. "Often the choir joined the congregation to swell its size."

Benjamin Rollins was appointed police chief when the town's original chief, Everett "Gunboat" Eldredge, retired. Rollins was the town's first patrolman, appointed in 1924, two years after Gunboat became chief.

Now that the war had ended, tourism could resume. "Despite a growing fear among some of the residents that the Cape is becoming too popular, it is evident that the Cape also retains an abundance of its old-fashioned color and peace," a *New York Times* travel writer proclaimed in 1947. Ludicrously, the writer asserted that Thoreau would not find the "over all picture" basically changed.[117]

Yet did tourism resume as before? If the whirligig maker Arthur Edwards, "Shavings," had served as the iconic "old salt" for an earlier generation of tourists eager to get to know "the real Cape," where was the old salt now? And did anyone care anymore? Actually, no. "The period after World War II saw the historical mythmaking on Cape Cod dissipate and an anything-goes approach emerge for attracting tourists."[118]

In the future, emphasis would be on nature as exemplified in the national seashore and the Cape's beaches. Cape Codders served merely as backdrops to the landscape and the beaches.

And of course, "then there is the often noted fact that the air on the Cape is different. The visitor immediately senses a fresh new quality, the quality noted on shipboard soon after leaving port." Many visitors would claim to sleep better in the sea air.

A Little Bit of a Letdown

"Snow had fallen, snow on snow, snow on snow, in the bleak mid-winter long ago," Christina Rossetti wrote in her 1872 hymn "In the Bleak Mid-Winter." Depending on how you saw it, Chatham could be happy or melancholy off-season. In the winter of 1948, Harold Dunbar painted the view from his window in the Old Village after a snowfall. The painting, which shows a solitary little girl dragging a sled up the road amid purple-blue shadows, conveys a kind of melancholy, suggesting that life has moved elsewhere. The Old Village is very quiet in the snow, even today.

In 1948, Walter and Katie Louchheim bought an 1820 house on Stage Harbor Road. Before the sale, the house's owner asked her neighbors "if they minded having a Jewish family nearby." Apparently, the neighbors' reaction was positive. Yet in years to come, it would rankle the Louchheims, avid tennis players, that the local tennis club refused to admit them.[119] President Lyndon Johnson named Louchheim deputy assistant secretary of state for educational and cultural affairs; eventually, the couple entertained eminent persons such as Minnesota senator Eugene McCarthy, who ran for president in 1968, and the poet W.H. Auden.[120]

Nothing but a "Little Shot-Gun Charge"

By 1949, World War II had been over for four years, yet if you were a resident of Chatham, you might be excused for thinking the war had never ended.

Virginia Crocheron Gildersleeve and Elizabeth Reynard were academics from Barnard College who retired together to Chatham.[121] Gildersleeve, who was born in 1877 in New York City, had spent her career at Barnard College as dean from 1911 to 1947; Reynard, twenty years her junior, was an associate professor of English.[122]

"The summers we spend on the lovely and spicy New England peninsula of Cape Cod in a house called Cahaba," Gildersleeve wrote in her 1954 memoir. Cahaba was a late eighteenth-century house perched on a small bluff overlooking the water. A couple of doors down from the painter Harold Brett's house, its wide lawn reached to the shore in a landscape dotted with firs, Cape pines, cedars, rhododendrons, roses and a small formal garden. "It had, also, the most beautiful willow in the world," Gildersleeve wrote in her foreword to *Cahaba*, a book of verses by Reynard that Gildersleeve published after Reynard's death.

In 1949, the two women and Reynard's elderly mother found themselves in this Eden, "stoically" enduring the roar of air force jet bombers dropping "token bombs on targets" on Monomoy.

If that wasn't bad enough, "the Air Force abruptly and dictatorially announced that it was extending the bombing area to just along the shore line, almost closing the harbor and ruining that part of the coast for fishing boats and sailing craft," Gildersleeve wrote.[123] The Thirty-third Fighter Wing, based at Otis Air Force Base, requested an additional 1.6 square miles of waters off Monomoy Point, where it would establish a surface bombing target danger zone.

The Chatham Board of Selectmen, demanding a meeting with air force officials, was rebuffed. Only when townspeople rose up and demanded the meeting did the air force relent. At this point, Gildersleeve, Reynard and Susan Brandeis organized the Women's Committee for the Protection of Chatham and rapidly collected signatures to protest the bombing zone.

The day of the public hearing came: September 1, 1949. "The big new hall was packed, with men and women standing against the wall at the back, and peering in the windows from outside," Gildersleeve recalled. A newspaper account estimates that the crowd in the Depot Street Community Building topped six hundred summer residents and year-rounders.

Present were Josephine Atkins, a lifelong Chatham resident; Clair L. Baisly, an architectural historian; the retired publisher Noble Cathcart and his daughter, Lucy Anne; Alice Guild; Virginia and Edith Harding; Minnie Buck's daughter, Josephine, and her husband, Professor Albert Ivanoff; Francis Jones, a trap fisherman; Doc Keene and his wife, Harriette; Walter Love, president of the Chatham Fisherman's Association; Justice Brandeis's daughter Elizabeth and her husband, Paul Raushenbush; and Alice Stallknecht's daughter-in-law, Joan Bingham Wight.

The hearing began at 2:20 p.m. with Colonel G.W. Carlson reading telegrams from Massachusetts senator Leverett Saltonstall and five representatives, including John F. Kennedy and John W. McCormack. None of the politicians favored expanding the bombing area.[124]

"On Monday afternoon, at 1:30, I was having lunch in the dining room," John W. Downes of Forest Beach Road, South Chatham, said during the hearing. "Bombing was going on to such an extent that the windows rattled, the house shook, the dishes fell over, and the pictures were askew on the wall." During the war, the military had practiced bombing at several coastal sites, including Camp Wellfleet, Nomans Land off Martha's Vineyard and Monomoy.[125] Wartime bombing was understandable even though Downes said that he used to watch "slap-happy" pilots buzzing the girls on the beach, "causing them many times to lay down in fear." But the war was over. (For decades after the war, beachgoers would find shells and unexploded ammunition.)

Incredibly, in this community based on fishing and beach tourism, the military was not only practicing firing machine guns toward targets on Monomoy, but it was also deep diving toward four targets on the island and using practice bombs, "either a nine-pound bomb with a little shotgun charge to show location or a 100-pound bomb." The previous summer, a P-47 Thunderbolt jet had crashed on Monomoy Point, killing the pilot, Edward W. Meacham. Yet in the future, the military expected to integrate rockets into its program.

"Nobody travels for rest and recreation to a place where, as Mr. Downes has told you, the dishes fall off the cupboards, the pictures go askew, and other damage is done," said state senator Edward C. Stone, who had traveled "all night" (although he lived about thirty miles distant, in Osterville) to attend the meeting.

Packed with people as it was, the room must have been getting stuffy as residents listened with growing incredulity to the military's plans.

"Can't the practice bombing be done somewhere else?" speaker after speaker wanted to know.

Even if a bomb, bullet or rocket might not actually hit and kill a beachgoer, "it might stop them from coming here for their recreation in the summertime if they found that was a bombing area," Representative Donald W. Nicholson said.

"There are other things, naturally, we would prefer and a bombing area is nothing that is, in my opinion, conducive to vacationers or summer residents," Senator Stone said, adding that 75 percent of Chatham's residents depended, in whole or in part, on the summer trade.

Testimony revealed that the military had riddled the roof of a member of the Ryder family with bullets and shot up the old Monomoy Lighthouse, now owned by George S. Bearse. The Stone Horse lightship was strafed. "They even machine gunned the fish traps," said F.E. Claflin.

Summer resident John W. Hutchinson of Concord said that he was sailing when he accidentally ventured into the forbidden zone. "I had five people aboard and it would not have added to our pleasure to be in a bombing area at that time," he said. He was eventually picked up by the Coast Guard.

Dave Ryder, president of Chatham's fishermen, said Chatham's $1 million fishing industry would be harmed.

"After coming back in this area after serving in two theaters of war, I could never understand why the Air Force was still so interested in this crowded area here," said Commander N.S. Gilchrist, U.S. Navy Reserve. "They have vast areas elsewhere in this country."

Nicholson raised the specter of communism on the eve of Senator Joe McCarthy's witch hunts for Communists:

> *There is probably not a Communist in Chatham. If there is, I don't believe anyone would pay any attention to him anyway. That is the kind of people you propose to take certain rights away from. If this was war time, you wouldn't find anyone in Chatham or anywhere else kicking up a stink about it.*

At the end of the meeting, Carlson "smiled faintly and asked whether anyone wished to speak in favor of the Army's proposal. There was another silence, then a loud, jeering yet good-natured laugh," Gildersleeve wrote.[126]

A few days later, the *Cape Cod Standard-Times* reported that the military was conducting a survey "to determine if the national interest requires military use of the area."

Eventually, it determined that the national interest could be served otherwise. The military found another bombing range. No longer was the sound of exploding bombs a constant backdrop to Chatham.

HAPPY NEW YEAR

And so, as the bloody, violent decade ended, it was quiet on Monomoy as the waters lapped the shore. It was a Saturday night, and not far away, on the mainland, revelers celebrated the end of the 1940s with champagne and noisemakers. The moon was waxing toward full, spilling white over the cold waters. Who would think that only months before military jets had streaked low over this quiet old place, dropping bombs? Who would think that in the two decades to come, bloody verbal battles would be fought over these sands?

Old Cape Cod

If you're fond of sand dunes and salty air,
Quaint little villages here and there,
You're sure to fall in love with
Old Cape Cod.
—*Claire Rothrock, Milton Yakus and Allan Jeffrey, 1957*

SUMMER AT THE SHORE

It began with a searing pain in the throat. Sixteen-year-old Jan Woolf was standing in her attic room at the Hawes House, a guesthouse on Main Street, sipping orange juice from a can when her throat suddenly contracted, as though she had just swallowed a sour grapefruit. Perhaps, too, she had a vague headache and felt hot—symptoms she might have attributed to getting too much sun at the beach on her day off.[127]

It was an awkward time to take sick. This was the height of the summer tourist season, and Jan was waitressing up here with Nancy Husted, her best friend from back home in New Jersey.

In the 1930s, Nancy's parents had discovered Hawes House, where they now stayed every summer for a couple of weeks. When Jan and Nancy became teenagers, they thought it would be fun to come up on their own and spend the summer working by the beach. Nancy signed on at the Hawes House when she was nearly fifteen and spent five summers there. Jan joined her for about three of those summers, starting in 1951.

Waitresses at the Hawes House on Main Street in the Old Village. Accommodations were not fancy, but guests who glanced out their bedroom windows at the Atlantic sparkling close at hand were hooked. *Photo courtesy of William and Nancy Koerner.*

In 1882, Zenas and Selena Hawes opened their boardinghouse on the corner of Main and Water Streets in the Old Village when Zenas retired from a life at sea. In the early days, the house had neither running water nor electricity. In 1912, their daughter, Eva, and her husband, Isaac Howes—with marriage Eva changed but one letter in her name—took over the inn. Eventually, the inn expanded from one building to a row of three on Water Street, with the lowest right on the Atlantic. By the time Jan and Nancy were waitresses, a third generation, Freeman and his wife, Lucille, were running the inn.

By the 1950s, Hawes House was among the oldest lodging establishments in town. It would run for another twenty years until a fourth generation of family members elected not to devote their careers to it. Times were changing, too. People craved more luxuries and perhaps less of a family atmosphere than the Hawes House provided.

Alice Stallknecht painted Eva and Ike Howes into her mural *Every Man to His Trade*. Eva and Ike stand beneath a small sign that says Hawes House. To the left and right of the sign are small cameo portraits of Selena and Zenas Hawes. Sketched in profile at the side of the painting are Freeman, Lucille and their daughter, Linda.

The Hawes House wasn't for everyone, but those who stayed swore by it. There was nothing fancy about the guest rooms lighted by a bare bulb dangling from the ceiling. A 7:30 a.m. bell rousted guests from sleep every morning. Hawes House seemed even more primitive when compared to the pampered luxury available up the street at the Chatham Bars Inn or to the comfort of the Hawthorne, the Mattaquasson or the Old Harbor Inn. Just around the corner on Main Street were the venerable Wayside and Cranberry Inns. But guests who glanced out their bedroom windows at the Atlantic sparkling close at hand were hooked. Weekly rates were reasonable. The home cookin' was good.

"Cape Cod food is hale and hearty, plain and plenty," the travel writer Eleanor Early wrote in 1949. "Chowders and stews and johnny cake. And for dessert, shortcakes and pies and Indian pudding. Baked beans on Saturday night, and fish balls for breakfast Sunday."[128]

And the funny thing was, most of the time back then the sun did shine, Nancy remembered many years later.[129]

The three buildings could accommodate about seventy guests. Families made a point of booking the same weeks each summer. The July crowd was generally younger and sillier than the older, richer August crowd, Nancy thought. Unlike at the cottage colonies down Route 28, families took their home-cooked meals at assigned seats at long tables of ten or twelve in the dining room. The six waitresses wearing cotton dresses, small white aprons (which they made themselves from a pattern provided by Lucille), saddle shoes and hairnets served breakfast promptly at 8:00 a.m. and, when breakfast was finished, tidied up the guests' bedrooms.[130] While each room had its own sink, the toilet was at the end of the floor, and the shower was outside. Sheets were changed once a week. If the girls were quick, they could dawdle on the beach for an hour before serving lunch.

Lifelong friendships began at Hawes House. Because so many of the families hailed from New Jersey, the families would sometimes socialize in the winter, back home. Most of the families had a designated Cape Cod box, too, ready for packing in the car next summer. Electrical wiring at Hawes House was primitive, and everything you used was run off an outlet in the ceiling. So the box might contain a plug with plenty of outlets, extension cords, bottle openers, jiggers and cocktail shakers. Alcohol was not served at the Hawes House, and people used to sneak into their rooms before dinner to have a drink. Eventually, this loosened up to guests hosting cocktail parties on the porch. A couple who rented the corner room in July used to put a block of ice in their sink, stick in an ice pick and open the window. By setting out mixers, the sink became an instant wet bar where guests mixed those favorite '50s cocktails: martinis, gin and tonics and J&B Scotch on the rocks right through the window.[131] But alcohol was never, ever consumed in the dining room.

For the guests, the days passed in a relaxing blur of shopping, fishing, boating and lolling around on the beach. It was possible then, before the dramatic erosion of the shoreline, to walk back from the fish pier along the beach. Sometimes in the evening, the guests might ask the waitresses to get up a beach party, and everyone would sit around a bonfire roasting hot dogs and singing. On a rare rainy day, guests would assemble in an otherwise shunned living room to smoke and work on jigsaw puzzles by the fireplace.

Back home in New Jersey during the winter, the girls would talk about finding higher-status, better-paying jobs up Shore Road the following summer. But then come March, they'd realize they loved Hawes House and would sign on for another season.

As her throat continued to ache, Jan decided to consult a local doctor. He made an unpleasant diagnosis: mumps.

Mumps? Who got mumps in the summer? No one else had mumps. Someone unknown at the movies must have spread mumps, the girls later decided. Jan was quarantined in the attic.

No more waiting tables, and she had to subsist on a soft, bland diet. Luckily, Nancy had already had mumps, so she was able to nurse Jan through her miserable days.

From the window in that garret, Jan could peek at the Atlantic. It had to be maddening to feel ill, trapped in quarantine, while everyone else was having fun in the sun.

William Koerner was one of the boys from New Jersey who came to Hawes House every summer with his parents. By the 1950s, Bill was a veteran of the place, having first arrived in 1938 or 1939. Bill took on the task of running shuffleboard contests at the court that overlooked the water. He'd collect one dollar from whoever was playing and then pay off the winner. As he entered his late teens, Bill was ready for more sophisticated entertainment,

William Koerner, who began visiting Hawes House with his parents in the late 1930s, took on the task of running shuffleboard contests at the court that overlooked the water. *Photo courtesy of William and Nancy Koerner.*

and he found ready dates in the seven waitresses employed each summer. (Bill eventually married Nancy.)

The waitresses casually dated local boys, too. If they went out in the evening, they hung an elastic band on the inside doorknob of the main door to the street. Freeman Howes would not lock that door until the last band had been removed from the knob.

One summer, someone found an old toilet that had lost its back. The toilet bowl seems to have begun its peculiar second career on Morris Island, but then it migrated along the shore until it landed not far from the Hawes House. Both Jan and Nancy were invited to beach parties where the lure was orange blossoms—gin and orange juice—served from the toilet. Jan assumed this was a joke until she saw the toilet punch bowl in action.

It is possible that the young man who introduced the toilet as a punch bowl was Robert Worth Bingham III. Worth, as he was known, was a member of Harvard's class of '54. His parents, Barry and Mary Bingham, owned the *Courier-Journal* and the *Louisville Times* newspapers and had been renting in Chatham for several summers. Worth had been expelled from Exeter for drinking and was something of a roué. According to one biography,

In their free time, the Hawes House waitresses saw movies on Main Street, attended Friday evening band concerts, bought ice cream at the Sad Sack Snack Shack and, of course, played on the beach. *Photo courtesy of William and Nancy Koerner.*

Worth threw a beach party using an old toilet as a punch bowl, "ladling out refreshments in a grand mockery of Louisville debutante balls."[132]

People were cutting loose. After the tension and rationing of the war years, once again life was free and easy. Those who had gone off to fight were back home again, and, for the most part, women returned to what was seen as their rightful place—the home. Gasoline was no longer rationed. It was time to settle down, make a few babies and take a vacation by the shore. Sometimes those vacationers liked Chatham so much that they decided to make it their home.

US AND THEM

One of the easiest ways to integrate into Chatham was to marry. Still, even spouses took a lot of ribbing, particularly if they came from somewhere away from the seashore and didn't know a clam from a quahog. To the Cape

Codder, "a clam is a clam and a quahaug is a quahaug," Joseph Lincoln once wrote.[133] "The distinction between the two is something that the Cape Cod child learns at his mother's knee—or at her table."

Virginia Harding married for the second time on October 11, 1951—one day after what would have been her ninth wedding anniversary with Arthur Durkee. Virginia's new husband was Thomas Joseph McGrath, a World War I veteran who ran a print shop in Chatham from 1948 to 1962. Edith Harding announced the marriage of her forty-three-year-old daughter to the sixty-four-year-old McGrath on plain, cream-colored card stock. This time, the couple would move into their own home, albeit around the corner from Edith, who would die two years after her daughter's marriage. Virginia's marriage would last until McGrath's death in January 1963.

When people speak about Chatham, it always comes down to "us and them," natives and summer people. Or sometimes a triad: natives, summer people and tourists. The military's presence in the 1940s had no doubt shaken up society a bit.

By the early 1950s, as the Cape was vigorously marketed as a retirement community, many, many newcomers were arriving and trying to make their way in what still seemed to outsiders a closed society.

At about that time, the writer Scott Corbett, his wife, Elizabeth, and young daughter, Florence, moved to East Dennis, fifteen miles or so up the road from Chatham. Corbett, a World War II veteran, had been living in a brownstone in New York City, and the family moved to Dennis, "a cemetery with lights," as people told him it would be, to try something different. They had no family ties on the Cape.

"He had been warned before moving to the Cape that Cape Codders were a cold bunch and that it could be six months before anyone even nodded to him."[134] At that time, the social life in Dennis was probably much like that in Chatham. Dennis was dominated by members of the Sears family, all of whom were related to one another in some complex way, just as Chatham was dominated by the Nickersons and the Eldredges.

Yet the Corbetts were accepted into this new society. As he told the Orleans Rotary Club at the end of 1953, after his book *We Chose Cape Cod*, an account of the family's experience, was published, Cape Codders rejected only those who acted superior or threw their weight around.

The Corbetts had been fed the old canard that snow never amounted to much on Cape Cod. But then it began to snow—and snow and snow. In a new subdivision in Chatham on Eldredge's Neck, one resident remembered the winter of 1951–52 as "a humdinger." Vallie Davis

Metcalf, a pioneer in Harbor Coves, was stranded for five days with no electricity, no pump and no water.

"They carried salt water from Crow's Pond to flush toilets and, using bottled gas, melted snow for fresh water. The house was very cold and damp."[135]

Eldredge's Neck and Nickerson's Neck stick out like two hands cupping Crows Pond. To the south of Eldredge's Neck is Ryder's Cove, and to the north of Nickerson's Neck is Pleasant Bay. In 1889, a Nickerson conveyed Nickerson's Neck, Eldredge's Neck and Strong Island to the Chatham Real Estate Trust for $5,000, and eleven years later, after a series of conveyances, H. Fisher Eldredge bought the one hundred or so acres of Eldredge's Neck for $450.

Fisher, born in 1851, was thirteen years the junior of his only brother, Marcellus. The pair came from solid Chatham stock—their father was Heman Eldredge and their mother, Mary Harding. The family summered in the house Mary grew up in on Main Street in the Old Village and spent the remainder of the year in Portsmouth, where Heman struck it rich with a beer brewery.

In 1900, after Fisher acquired Eldredge's Neck, he built a cottage and a vast stable. As he and his wife, Addie, planned to entertain, he built a dance pavilion. He also built a carriage shed, a corncrib and a private icehouse.

During the Great War, Fisher's daughter Sadie hosted twice-weekly dances for the servicemen at the U.S. Naval Air Station around the corner on Nickerson's Neck. In 1925, she bought out her sister Nettie's share of the estate, and the large estate sat vacant except for the occasional rumrunner who stashed his liquor on the beach below Fisher's bungalow. But all that would change dramatically after World War II, when "a boom ensued on Cape Cod that has not abated."[136]

A GOOD SPOT FOR NECKING

Anyone trying to nap in Chatham on a summer's afternoon in the 1950s might be in for a shock. Except for the oldest parts of town, like the Old Village, that were already built up, the background noise of Chatham was a rumble of bulldozers and a whine of chainsaws. Everywhere you looked, developers were cutting swaths through the piney woods. Drivers had to crawl by construction sites, where the pickup trucks belonging to construction gangs were pulled half off the road surface into muddy gulches. Enormous trucks piled high with lumber inched through town. The sound of hammering split the air.

Tour Chatham sometime and ask yourself: which of these houses was built after World War II? An easier question is: which of these houses was built *before* World War II? Soon, you begin to get an idea of how, well, *empty* Chatham looked until the 1950s.

In 1948, Fisher's daughter Sadie sold Eldredge's Neck to Harbor Coves, Inc., which was owned by several members of the Smythe family of Palm Beach, Florida. Within a couple of months, developer A. Burns Smythe had surveyed ninety-six lots and a new road and, after printing up a sales brochure with a drawing of a windmill on the cover, was ready to begin selling lots. This was only the start.

As veterans returned from World War II, an unprecedented building boom took off. "By 1960, one-quarter of all American housing was new, built in the previous decade."[137] Levittown on Long Island inaugurated the idea of suburbia, and throughout the '50s, the key to Chatham would be subdivision.

The year 1955 was the biggest one for approvals since 1950, with eleven subdivisions with 282 lots and twenty-five private roads being approved. The look of the town changed with each subdivision. In fact, between 1950 and 1960, Chatham's population would rise by nearly 50 percent.

"It's growth. The Cape is growing. Countless new dwellings and business places are being erected. Thus far it doesn't seem to be a wild development but just a steady, constant growth," a page-one column in the *Cape Codder* proclaimed on February 16, 1950. "Anyone who looks around can see the increase of new enterprise in the business scheme. 'Outsiders' are coming in and stimulating new ideas and new trends."

The newspaper concluded, "It's the new blood, largely, that is building Cape Cod."

The building boom was partly attributable to "new, easier regulations and more favorable financing restrictions."[138] In mid-September 1951, one Cape Cod builder said he had observed a "noticeable surge."

The Cook and Learnard families lived near each other in Newton and vacationed together, too. Gould and Helen Cook, known as Brud and Crum, were the parents of Cinnie, Pril and Joe. Ted and Bea Learnard were the parents of Ann, Sandy and Barbie. For several years, the adults and their six children rented houses close to each other in Chatham, but by August 1949, they were ready to buy their own houses. Avid golfers, they wanted to own property convenient to Eastward, Ho! Country Club on Nickerson's Neck. So the two families bought lots across from each other on brand-new Seapine Road in Harbor Coves and built their houses.

During the '50s Eastward, Ho! was actively soliciting new members by mailing invitations describing the club's benefits and enclosing applications. In 1950, an annual golf membership for men over thirty was $140; for men under thirty and ladies it was $95. Social memberships were about half that.[139]

In the early days, the road into Harbor Coves was dirt. There were "no trees to speak of," and the houses enjoyed an unobstructed vista over to Fox Hill, Strong Island and the outer beach. "We could also see over Nickerson's Neck...and into Pleasant Bay," Barbie Learnard-Chase recalled in 2003.[140]

For the six young people, this undeveloped part of Chatham was paradise. They held beach parties on Fox Hill and water-skied on Crow's Pond at night. One bluff was known as "a favorite 'after-hours' spot for parkers." They learned to drive in an open Jeep on Fisher Eldredge's "open, grassy and very bumpy" old farm.

"A chubby and cheery cube of a man" named Mike Stello lived in the windmill overlooking Crow's Pond. In 1950, the well-known Chatham boat designer F. Spaulding Dunbar had reconditioned the windmill, and now Stello acted as caretaker for the enormous property. Learnard-Chase remembered that the kids loved to examine the little machine Stello used to make his own pasta.

SOMEONE TO TUG ON THE REINS

It has often been remarked that just as Patti Page was singing about Cape Cod's "winding roads that seem to beckon you," those same roads were being bulldozed to make way for houses and more houses.

Early in 1949, the town created a five-member planning board, and a year later that board approved ten new subdivisions with 257 lots and nineteen new roads. "Town Planning simply means the guiding of future, sound and orderly growth in an effort to make Chatham a better place in which to live and to maintain its inherent charm," the board said in its 1950 *Report of the Town Officers.*

In 1950 and 1951, 401 building permits were issued worth $1,363,960. "We cannot stop the wheels of progress," the board intoned in 1952. "We can only guide their direction to a certain extent. Our problem today is one of protection. The protection of Chatham's character, her natural attractiveness and her most valuable resources." Naturally, with growth came unwanted consequences. "The rapid growth of some commercial areas of the Town, stores and street widening have brought about the destruction of

Selectman Sabin "Slim" Hutchings at his Texaco gas station, 1950s. Hutchings typified the independent Cape Codder who fiercely opposed zoning and planning laws. He is remembered today as the model for Christ in Alice Stallknecht's murals. *Photo courtesy of the Chatham, Massachusetts Historical Society.*

many shade trees, which it is hoped this program will begin to replace," the board wrote in 1956.

But the problem ran deeper than simple protection. "Cape Codders are always conscious and irked by Government regulation," a columnist wrote in the *Cape Codder* on February 16, 1950. "Cape Cod's independence is deeply rooted and the proponents for Town planning, building codes or zoning must also give that due attention."

Today, we remember Slim Hutchings as the tall, skinny, hollow-cheeked model for Alice Stallknecht's Christ figures. The proprietor of a North Chatham gas station, "Slim Hutchings's Garage—Wreck and Ruin—Poverty Flat," Slim was elected to the board of selectmen in 1955 and served until 1960. During that time, he emerged as a fierce and outspoken opponent of planning and zoning, at one point threatening to call a special town meeting to defeat measures approved at a previous meeting.

The February 1950 town meeting was "one of the hottest town meetings on record." A cadre made a motion to throw out the planning board that voters at the 1949 town meeting had elected. Slim "touched off the fuse of the anti-planners" during the meeting held in the movie theatre. "Throughout, in the talk of the opponents, there seemed to be an underlying fierce regard for private rights."[141]

Yet after all the rhetoric died down, voters failed to disassemble the planning board. In the words of the *Cape Codder* columnist, "Let's have 'healthy' growth. Lots of it."

Again at the 1952 town meeting—now moved to the school auditorium, which seated five hundred—Slim tried to lead a faction to chuck out the planning board. He was again unsuccessful. The town did accept the old railroad station from Phyllis Graves Cox, which it would eventually convert to a museum. And the town voted to add buoys to mark the channel between Aunt Lydia's Cove and Chatham Bars.

That same month ground was broken for the first of thirty-eight houses to be built at "Stillwaters." The subdivision was named for Stillwater Pond, just off of Old Comers Road in Chatham Port, near the site of the radio station. The plans called for "Cape Cod architecture" geared to attract medium-priced buyers. "It is a development of which Cape Cod, and Chatham in particular, can well be pleased."[142]

Cape Cod architecture. That phrase no doubt evoked something specific to those who heard it in the 1950s—perhaps weathered cedar shingles and a modest but snug house. "The Cape Cod cottage is the nearly perfect house," one architectural historian writes.[143] With its one and a half stories, gable roof and big central chimney, it was low enough and snug enough to withstand Cape Cod's sand- and snowstorms.

The Cape was an indigenous architectural form that grew out of the English timbered house. In the 1920s, the "newly reborn Cape" became a staple of Colonial revival architecture. But by the 1950s, the Cape was "firmly established as a mainstay of subdivision developments across the country."[144] It was, in fact, "the most popular domestic design."[145]

Boston architect Royal Barry Wills, who was trained at MIT and began his career in 1919, "produced hundreds of always-identifiable houses featuring the massive chimney and an authentic early Cape façade."[146] Some of his houses stand in Chatham today.

By 1954, the planning board was boasting in the *Report of the Town Officers* of the tremendous cooperation between builders and the board. In five years, the board disapproved only two plans for subdivisions. Zoning was still in the future.

WE'VE GOT TO STOP THOSE HOT DOGS

Hot dogs. Hot dog stands. People who eat hot dogs. These monstrosities are the byproducts of an unregulated society. Some day you might wake to find a hot dog stand firmly parked at the edge of your property—and how would you like that?

Again and again, both at town meetings and in columns about the direction of Chatham and its lack of zoning, the specter of hot dogs is invoked.

"No one should have the right to open a hot dog stand, a gas station or a restaurant in a residential area," Judge Benjamin P. Gallanti of New Jersey, who said he traveled three hundred miles every summer to stay in Chatham, told a crowd to booming applause.[147]

In 1929, a couple named Szempleski had, in fact, opened a hot dog stand on Hardings Beach Road. A shack, really, they called it the Beach Galley, and it operated until it was lost in the 1938 hurricane. After that, the family opened a restaurant, the Sou'wester, up Barn Hill Road on Route 28.

Bland hot dogs, which had their origins in spicy German sausages, had been consumed in buns in America since the late nineteenth century. By the early twentieth century, hot dogs were associated with baseball, and by the late 1920s, wienie roasts were all the rage. It's not that Chatham residents didn't eat hot dogs; but generally, when they did so, they called them wienies and frankfurters.

The words "hot dog" were fighting words, especially when coupled with the word "stand." As early as the early 1930s, editorialists in the *Cape Cod Standard-Times* had been carping about "unsightly hot dog stands" dotting the once-quaint Cape. In 1937, Harold Dunbar opposed a Cape Cod Advancement Plan that called for advertising. "Who would profit?" he asked. Barkeepers, gas stations, cheap souvenir shops and "hot-dog stands."[148] That same year, the *Boston Evening Transcript* ran an editorial warning that a Mid-Cape highway would encourage "Coney Island sort of joints."

And everyone knew what the menu was on Coney Island: hot dogs.

In 1939, when President and Mrs. Franklin D. Roosevelt announced they would serve hot dogs to King George VI at a Hyde Park picnic, hot dogs were fully Americanized. Although the president's mother was "scandalized—like much of America" that the first lady planned to serve the royals hot dogs, plans went ahead. Franklin Jr. presented a hot dog on a silver platter to Queen Elizabeth. "How do you eat it?" she asked the president. "Very simple," Roosevelt answered. "Push it into your mouth and keep pushing until it is all gone."[149]

"By now, [hot dogs] had taken on mythic power as the great symbol of democracy."[150]

And that, in effect, was the problem with hot dogs. They were democratic. Originally sold by immigrants, some still detected a whiff of steerage about them. They represented the melting pot. They were popular on Coney Island, everyone's favorite example of a honky-tonk beach resort gone mad. Chatham was, after all, a higher-toned resort than Coney Island, which catered to the masses on a hot summer's day. And so even if a Chatham resident liked a wienie now and then, hot dog stands had to be kept in their place—the ballpark, Coney Island. Chatham had no patience for the hot dog stand; it had to be zoned out.

And what about zoning? There was none as yet.

In March 1938, Harold Dunbar had harped on the dangers of the town's lack of zoning, warning against people "selling their souls for a hot dog stand." In prose parodying Gertrude Stein, he wrote, "We want independence you can regulate the other guy but not me what do I care for the town, own the property I don't know nothing about zoning." Thus Dunbar accurately encapsulated the argument against zoning.[151]

"We just hope Chatham will grow gradually," Richardson Wright, who retired to Chatham, wrote in his regular *Cape Codder* column, "Chatham on the Half Shell," on October 15, 1953. "Maybe we should take a more serious view on zoning. Without it Chatham could soon enough acquire the honky tonk atmosphere which has ruined the road from Bass River to Hyannis."

Finally, four months later, in February 1954, "the Chatham old guard fell back in stunning defeat in Monday's annual town meeting as motion after motion of the newer voters in that town carried. Zoning was voted through 140–120."[152] The victory was slim, but zoning was now a reality, although three years later, the zoning rules were still being hotly debated. Chatham's summer residents, who did not have a vote in town affairs, still held their own summer town meeting, where they spoke generally in favor of zoning. One summer resident said he didn't want "noisy dance halls."

As resident Joseph Dubis observed, "People are for zoning if it helps them and against it if it hurts them. I have yet to see an objective viewpoint."

Slim Hutchings fought zoning as zealously as he had planning. "Every inch of Massachusetts is a battleground," he said. "There is no such thing as a purely residential area."

MID-CAPE HIGHWAY

"If you drive from the ship canal to Provincetown any time from Memorial Day to Labor Day you are likely to think that Cape Cod is only a long and crooked sun resort," wrote a book reviewer in the *New York Times* on June 4, 1951. "Automobiles crawl bumper to bumper, tourist traps flourish and vacationists display their sunburn in square foot sections."

After the war, the Cape was exploding with people in their cars speeding along the new highway, "the most significant influence on the Cape's development."[153]

"If Cape Cod's old roads are beautiful, the new, in their way, are more so," one writer proclaimed in 1972.[154] "Broad and unspoiled, they slice through where no trail existed before."

In 1949, the state allocated $100 million for highway construction.[155] The following year, a "two-lane limited access Mid-Cape Highway, from the Sagamore Bridge to the West Barnstable Rotary at Exit 6," opened. In 1950, construction of a single-lane Mid-Cape to Route 132 had been completed, and holidays on the Fourth of July and Labor Day broke traffic records.

Provincetown selectman Charles Mayo recalls seeing cars stop on Route 6 and "businessmen get out with briefcases and walk through the brush." Those men were, of course, scoping out sites for subdivisions and commercial buildings. The Mid-Cape spurred "what many were beginning to term the 'ruination' of the lower Cape."[156]

On December 29, 1953, a twelve-mile "double barreled link" opened from the Sagamore Bridge to Barnstable. With the highway, development and tourism soared. Through the remainder of the decade, the road crept steadily toward what would be its stopping point, the Orleans Rotary, and, in some areas, expanded to four lanes.

While the Mid-Cape Highway encouraged development down the center of the Cape, away from the two shores, and made travel down the length of the Cape quicker and easier, it soon proved to be a double-edged sword. The 1953 highway death toll of twenty tripled the previous year's. While it was now "almost essential" to have a car "to thoroughly appreciate and enjoy a Cape Cod vacation,"[157] the car might actually hurt the Cape's tourist industry. "If the accident and death rate should continue to rise as it has the Cape resort business will suffer in the opinion of those who have asked what can be done about this alarming situation." The writer quoted a Cape Codder as saying, "The few—very few—crazy drivers are scaring the considerate motorist off the roads."

Yet the relentless progress of the road could not be halted. In April 1954, piers for the Mid-Cape to cross over Willow Street in Yarmouth were under construction. In 1955, Chatham's planning board called for a study of the approach to the new Mid-Cape Highway via Route 137. The exit 11 overpass was completed in 1955. By 1959, two lanes had been completed from Dennis to the rotary in Orleans. (In 1967 and 1971, further phases of construction would complete the four-lane divided highway as far as exit 9 in Dennis.)[158]

A LAST, DESPERATE GAME OF CARDS

Looting. After any shipwreck, the rumor mill grinds into action, and the wreck of the SS *Pendleton* on February 18, 1952, in sixty-foot seas about five miles off Chatham, was no exception.

The story went that after the tanker broke in half, the men were playing a "last, desperate" game of cards in the stern as they waited for their rescuers. The stakes grew. But then someone reminded the players of a "sea going superstition that says the man who picked up the stakes would fall victim to the sea." Who would dare to take his winnings? "No one picked up the money and there existed a sizeable pot of cash for the looters, according to the stories which passed from person to person."[159]

The thrilling story of the Coast Guard's heroic rescue of men from the *Pendleton* has passed into legend and been told again and again. "The operation was a modern version of the exploits of old time surfmen who manned stations along the Outer Cape and thrilled the natives with their heroism."[160]

The day began with a fierce blizzard. The winter of 1952 had already been a harsh one, and now, with the fresh snow, "the local people were busy digging out of the snow that invaded them," Boatswain's Mate First Class Bernard Webber remembered.[161] For the Coast Guard men at the Chatham station, the day was busy. In the morning, they learned that the tanker SS *Fort Mercer* had broken in half about forty miles out to sea from Chatham. Local fishermen, too, needed help as their boats broke away from their moorings in the harbor.

The station's resources were stretched thin, and the men were cold and exhausted by mid-afternoon when they learned that the 534-foot tanker SS *Pendleton*, loaded with eleven thousand gallons of kerosene and heating oil, had also broken in two.

At 5:55 p.m., in darkness and with cold snow biting their faces, Webber and a three-man crew set out from the Chatham Fish Pier in the motorboat *CG 36500*.[162] During the next grueling hours, Webber and his crew would save thirty-two of the thirty-three men in the *Pendleton*'s stern. A Jacob's ladder missing the penultimate rung dangled from the boat's starboard quarter. One by one, the men descended the ladder and jumped into the lifeboat. Webber's crew plucked out of the frigid waters those who missed.

Jacob's ladder. The name is taken from a dream of Jacob in the book of Genesis in which Jacob sees angels ascending and descending a ladder to heaven. This was a marine ladder made of rope or chain with wooden rungs. The ladder would probably haunt the nightmares of the men involved for years to come.

The final passenger was Ordinary Seaman George Myers, "Tiny." For a moment, Tiny hung on the Jacob's ladder, 350 pounds of him, nearly naked. When he jumped, he missed, and the seas rapidly crushed him between the *CG 36500* and the *Pendleton*. "I felt sick to my stomach over the loss of Tiny," Webber later said.

The trip back was as harrowing as the trip out. At the fish pier, "I looked up and was overwhelmed by the crowd standing there—men, women and even children of Chatham had turned out on this stormy night to greet and aid the survivors."

"Please direct me to the road to drive to the *Pendleton*" was for many years a common request at the Chatham Information Booth on Main Street. The Blizzard of '78 submerged most of the hulk; the following summer, the government detonated it. *Photo by the author.*

At the Coast Guard station, the men were attended by doctors and clergymen. Ben Shufro, manager of the Puritan Clothing Store, measured the men for dry uniforms. "All I wanted was a cup of coffee and a good Cushman's doughnut," Webber wrote.

Webber slept at the station, and the next morning when he woke, he saw money lying on his floor. His bureau drawer was open, and money cascaded from it, too. Money, money everywhere—and he had no idea where it came from. Downstairs, he learned that the men on the *Pendleton* had taken up a collection. Eventually, the money would be used to buy a television set for the station—"a luxury unheard."

The much-lauded quartet was known later as the "Gold Crew." All four men were awarded Congressional Gold Lifesaving Medals.

For twenty-six years, the bow of the *Pendleton* remained visible off Chatham. "Inflated rumors of its value swirled around town for years, like Chatham fog," Dana Eldridge wrote.[163] Eldridge and his friends once concocted a scheme to raise it using ping-pong balls.

"Please direct me to the road to drive to the *Pendleton*," had become, by 1956, a common request among the nearly nineteen thousand annual inquiries at the Chatham Information Booth on Main Street.[164] The Blizzard of '78 submerged most of the hulk under water; during the summer of '79, the government declared the hulk a safety hazard and blew it up.

CHATHAM ON THE HALF SHELL

How do you make clams casino? Start with "good Chatham Little Necks still in the shell." Mix green peppers with an equal amount of onions and sauté. Spread on the little necks, top with a smidge of bacon and bake in a slow oven for twenty minutes.

"The clam goes straight from the shell into your mouth. Licking good."[165] So wrote Richardson Little Wright in his weekly *Cape Codder* column "Chatham on the Half Shell." Wright had lived, since 1950, on a high hill overlooking the Oyster River at the end of Barn Hill Road. There, he cultivated lilacs, roses and lilies and, fortunately for the readers of the *Cape Codder*, based seven miles down the road from Chatham in Orleans, wrote a column ostensibly about Chatham that was really a rumination on life, flowers, retirement, literature, women and food.

Wright was born in 1887 and, in 1914, assumed the editorship of *House & Garden Magazine*. He also wrote forty books, many of them on gardening.[166]

After retiring from the magazine in 1950, he and his third wife, Gertrude Albion McCormick, retired to "this windy and salubrious elbow of sand," where he continued writing until his death from a stroke in 1961.[167] The byline on "Chatham on the Half Shell" was actually "The Richardson Wrights," with Gertrude sharing credit.

During strawberry season in June, Wright recommended enhancing the berries with Kirsch. "Pour it with a steady, reluctant hand." He also recommended what he dubbed "estuary crawling"—sort of an automobile version of gunk holing whereby you drive the car to offbeat spots such as Cockle Cove at sunset. "Great places for lovers, these road-end estuaries and hidden old town landings."[168]

WHEN A HEADACHE ISN'T A HEADACHE

It began with a headache. A stiff neck. Fatigue. Nothing to worry about. But then, two days later, you were paralyzed and found yourself in a hospital, perhaps even encased in an iron lung with only your head sticking out.

It was infantile paralysis—poliomyelitis, "polio" for short—"the last of the great childhood plagues."[169] Polio is a virus that is actually an intestinal infection. While some may have a slight case and never know it, others suffer irreversible paralysis and, when breathing is affected, die.

"One night after supper I got up from the table and then fell down," recalls Alice Guild's grandson Gene, the youngest of three boys. It was 1942. His mother took Gene to the hospital, and the diagnosis was frightening: polio. The paralysis affected Gene's right leg.[170]

Yet Gene got off easily—he was given a fish scale to hook under a door and manipulate with his foot to get his muscles going. Another child in his class, whose right leg was also affected, wore a brace and had to sit at the sidelines during sports class. Gene recuperated and enjoyed school athletics.

"Epidemic diseases that strike whole communities at the same time are more frightening than chronic diseases that kill individuals over a number of years," one writer commented. "Diseases that strike the young and active are more terrible than those that prey upon the old and weak."[171]

Polio had first been seen in epidemic form in 1916. The following year in Chatham, a scourge of polio created a "feeling of unrest and fear among our inhabitants, especially the summer colony."[172] But the postwar polio epidemic was something new. Beginning in 1949, as the baby boom advanced, polio grew into an epidemic that could not be ignored. The "summer dread of paralysis" coupled with "new and horrible possibilities of nuclear holocaust and by the pervasive fear of Communist infiltration of the United States" created an atmosphere of doom.[173]

"Do you want to spend the rest of your life in an iron lung?" No? Then stay away from the beach. The pool. The movie theatre. The water fountain.

These words rang out in countless houses across Cape Cod in the warm months, from June to September, when the polio epidemic advanced. Gene's mother warned him and his brothers against swimming in ponds.

Hand in hand with polio came the founding of the March of Dimes, a charity that promised that, together, we can "strike out polio." An advertisement in the *Cape Cod Standard-Times* on January 11, 1951, pictured eight-year-old Barry Brown of Mesa, Arizona, in his baseball uniform. Barry had been stricken with polio when he was three. The gruesome specter of previously healthy toddlers now encumbered with wheelchairs and leg braces was an effective one.

During that summer of 1952, the worst year nationally for the polio epidemic, the Rogers & Gray Insurance Company in Orleans ran ads for polio insurance "as low as $10" in the *Cape Codder*. Making the ads sinister was a photo of a young girl resembling Shirley Temple—she could be next, the reader thinks.

While 1952 was the worst year nationwide for the polio epidemic, with fifty-seven thousand cases that would kill three thousand, Chatham reported two cases. In fact, 1949 had been the Cape's worst year, with twenty-five cases reported Cape-wide.[174] "In a few of the children infantile paralysis in a mild form has caused muscle weaknesses which might not have been discovered for a long while," the 1952 *Report of the Town Officers* said. "These are now being treated, some by the crippled children's Clinic, or elsewhere, with marked improvement."

Yet even as children died, researchers toiled at vaccines. In 1954, Jonas Salk began his polio vaccine trials, vaccinating two million elementary school children en masse, free of charge. An April 12, 1955 page-one, lead headline in the *Cape Cod Standard-Times* read, "Salk Vaccine 80–90 Percent Effective." In the summer of 1956, the polio vaccine was available to everyone under age twenty through private physicians.[175] By the end of the decade, vaccines, not polio, were the norm. "Everyone under forty is asked to avail himself of the free polio shots, being given by four doctors at the Fire House tomorrow from 2 to 8 p.m."[176] was a typical announcement.

A Poet, Incognito

August 17, 1952. Twilight in Kate Gould Park.

"Behind the black outlines of the pines there is the fading afterglow, translucent, golden, of the setting sun, and the circle around the bandstand is dark with crowds of people in the grass."[177]

So wrote a nineteen-year-old diarist from Wellesley who answered an ad in the *Christian Science Monitor* asking for a "neat, intelligent college-age girl of pleasing personality."[178] For six weeks that summer, the young woman was a mother's helper for the Cantor family, summer people on Bay Lane who practiced Christian Science.

The Chatham Band breaks into a Gershwin medley, beginning with a "jazzy version of 'Liza.'" The summer air smells of buttery popcorn. "For a mile around the cars are parked, and the people are all there in their summer suits and dresses—the old gray-haired couples, the old women in groups, like gentle lavender-scented butterflies, softly, slowly talking."

And the mother's helper has brought two of her charges, the Cantors' younger children, Susan and Billy, who are five and three. The three of them sit on a blanket in the dark, listening to the music and observing the children toddling around with balloons. The mother's helper is a Smith College student who will begin her junior year in a couple of weeks.

Her name is Sylvia Plath. One year and one week from now, she will unsuccessfully try to kill herself through an overdose of sleeping pills. This episode will form the climax of her novel *The Bell Jar*. She will successfully kill herself in London in 1963 by sticking her head in a gas oven. She will be awarded the Pulitzer Prize posthumously in 1982. But on this day, no one knows who she will become.

A few days later, Sylvia walks down Main Street with a date, looking at "all the summer people in their queer clothes—brown ladies in silk print dresses and ropes of white jewelry; girls in colored shorts—red, green, blue; bright tan faces, golden, bronze, pink, beige—all ripe with sun-color, moving easily and free in the summer sun."[179] That summer she goes on dates, dawdles at the beach, sails and writes in her diary.

One day she meets the novelist Val Gendron, who was working in Lorania's Bookmobile, an extension of a store in Hyannis that visited Chatham once a week. Val is eighteen years Sylvia's senior; a photo of Val shows a dark-haired woman with a round face and blood-red lipstick. Sylvia worships Val for being a published author, largely of westerns for the teenage reader, and visits her in her Dennis Port cottage.

After her 1956 marriage to Ted Hughes, Sylvia would return to Cape Cod. Hughes's poem "Flounders" describes a day the pair spent in a rowboat fishing off Chatham, probably during the summer of 1957, when they vacationed for seven weeks in Eastham. "Was that a happy day? From Chatham / Down at the South end of the Cape, our map / Somebody's optimistic assurance, / We set out to row." The pair is beached on a sandbar and saved by a powerboat. Near land, they pull up flounders "big as big plates." "How tiny an adventure / To stay so monumental in our marriage."[180]

COLORLESS, ODORLESS, TASTELESS RADIOACTIVE STUFF

It has perhaps been forgotten now, as we remember the 1950s in an *Ozzie and Harriet* glow, that this was a period of great stress. While World War II had been a straightforward, black-and-white conflict, the threats of the 1950s were more insidious and horrible. Think of polio germs in the swimming pool. Think of invisible radiation seeping into your house. Think of your child's teacher pledging himself to Joe Stalin.

This was early in the Cold War, when Senator Joe McCarthy was regularly churning up Communists.[181] Men were being drafted through the stepped-up Selective Service, and some, like Dana Eldridge of South Chatham, were sent to fight in Korea. When the Soviets exploded an atomic bomb, it seemed that the superpower was posing a threat that the United States was ill prepared to meet.

In 1950, the selectmen recommended that the town establish a permanent civil defense system. "Such a defense program in the event of a future war which might come to our shores would utilize the facilities and all the skill and energy of the civil defense workers," the 1950 *Report of the Town Officers* noted.

In 1951, Robert A. McNeece became the director of the civil defense committee; Doc Keene served as medical officer, and nine additional men headed other departments, including public relations. New seven-and-a-half-horsepower warning sirens were installed on Depot Road, and a rescue truck was rigged up as an ambulance. An auxiliary power plant in the town office had been tested during two power failures and worked fine.

Because Chatham had been declared a "Non Target Area," volunteers that fall made a door-to-door survey of Chatham's housing asking how

An aerial photo of the Cold War SAGE radar site on Stepping Stones Road. Many residents never knew that the top-secret site was there from 1953 to about 1960. *Photo courtesy of MITRE Corporate Archives, Bedford, Massachusetts.*

many people "the family would harbor in the event of an evacuation"[182] from a target area such as Boston.

In 1952, the group sponsored a blood-typing program and provided personnel with ID cards showing their fingerprints and photographs. "The lessening of the threat of imminent war had made possible the more deliberate and thorough study of defense problems with a resultant saving in effort and money," McNeece reported in the 1952 *Report of the Town Officers.*

At the same time Chatham was looking to protect itself, Cape Cod entered a larger system of radar protection. In the early 1950s, a long-range radar test site was erected in South Truro as a part of the experimental Semi-Automatic Ground Environment (SAGE) Sector. "The system used ground-based radars, sea-based radars on ocean platforms called Texas Towers, and airborne radars to detect enemy traffic."[183] The entire system extended from Montauk Point, Long Island, to West Bath, Maine, and included three long-range heavy radars, three height-finding radars and twelve gap-filler radars. The South Truro radar site had short-range blind spots and relied on "gap-filler radars" in Chatham and Sandwich. In 1952, the Chatham gap-filler

The Stepping Stones Road site today offers few clues as to its past as a gap-radar installation from 1953 to about 1960. *Photo by the author.*

radar was located near the site of the old World War II Army Air Forces radar station, on a hill just off Stepping Stones Road.

Lonnie Pickett Jr., who grew up near Stepping Stones Road and whose father was a World War II radar specialist, remembers the site.[184] "I can still hear the hum," Pickett said. Pickett and his friends used to gaze in through the chain-link fence at the facility. He recalls that three or four air force personnel manned the station, which consisted of two white flattop buildings and the radar array. "We were never allowed inside the fence."[185]

It is likely that Chatham's S-band radar unit was "assembled mostly from World War II components."[186] The Cape Cod system was fully operational by September 1953, and in the following years, at least five hundred flights were made to challenge it and collect operational and design data.[187]

Radar and radiation were buzzwords of the '50s. By 1956, the idea of shelters had come into question, as "they are not able to withstand the force of atomic and thermo-nuclear bombs." But by 1958, the state had developed a survival plan. Selectman Slim Hutchings and Director of Civil Defense Harold Claflin received instructions from the "Sector 2C headquarters" and also obtained two radiological monitoring sets at no charge.

Eventually, technology and politics moved on. The facility on Stepping Stones Road operated from 1953 until it became inactive sometime before 1960.

THE FLYING CHAUFFEUR

Chatham Municipal Airport had been steadily maturing alongside the new technology of aviation, and in 1950, the site was ready for "official acceptance." Air travel was deemed vital for civil defense. "Should it become necessary to move our entire population or a considerable part of the town's residents and their important possessions…we would find the Chatham Airport available and of great import in this transportation problem," said the 1950 *Report of the Town Officers*. "We being located in a seacoast town surely places us in a dangerous position in event of an invasion which we earnestly hope will never occur." By 1952, the airport's twenty-five-hundred-foot runway was "surrounded by smooth, well-cropped grass."

Wilfred Berube, a French Canadian chauffeur to the summer family the Shattucks, was a pioneer in early aviation. In the days before instruments, "he could fly anywhere just by following railroad tracks and never got lost."[188] In the '20s, Berube bought seventy-two acres of "completely unimproved land" in West Chatham from Josephine Hardy. "Stump-pulling, rock-pulling, smoothing, cultivating—Wilfred did all of it, working day and night for years to create what he calls Mon Reve or My Dream"[189]—an airport. He transformed the forest of scrub pines into open grassland suitable for a runway and erected a fifty- by sixty-five-foot airplane hangar. By the mid-'30s, private planes had begun flying into Chatham Airport. The airport closed for a period during World War II and then resumed after the war. The town bought the property in 1951.

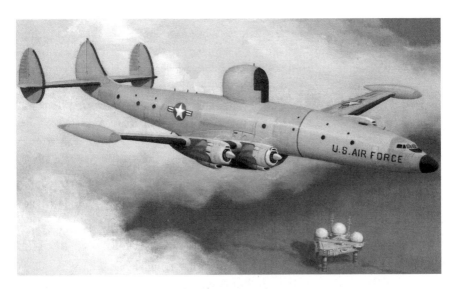

A painting of bomber over a Texas Tower. Texas Tower #2, one of three offshore radar sites augmenting the SAGE radar detection system, was located in the Atlantic Ocean 125 miles east of Chatham. Helicopters servicing the towers refueled at Chatham Airport. *Original painting by Lonnie Pickett Jr.*

The airport was also used for a serious Cold War purpose. Texas Tower #2, one of three offshore radar sites augmenting the SAGE radar detection system, was planted in the Atlantic Ocean about 125 miles east of Chatham. The Helicopter Operations Section of the 551st Air Base Squadron at Otis Air Force Base used Chatham Airport as a refueling point between Cape Cod and the Texas Tower. The helicopters serving the tower were "huge, banana-shaped twin-rotored" machines that hauled personnel, equipment and supplies back and forth to the tower—notorious gas guzzlers.[190]

Chatham is "a most vital point for the helicopters as it is the nearest refueling point to the Texas Tower and their 300 gallon tanks allow but a very small margin for safety when making these trips." How much fuel could they take on here? "Enough," says Lonnie Pickett, who manages Chatham Airport and has rendered the Texas Towers in oil paints.

In 1954, 511 helicopters supplied Texas Tower #2, according to the 1954 *Report of the Town Officers*. Berube was much lauded for serving coffee and refreshments to the weary pilots.[191]

A HERITAGE AT THE DUMP

On September 18, 1953, Harold Crocker Dunbar, "one of Cape Cod's most famous painters," died in Cape Cod Hospital thirty minutes after he arrived there.[192] He was seventy years old and had suffered from arteriosclerotic heart disease for ten years, according to his death certificate.

Two days later, he was buried at Seaside Cemetery. His first wife, Brownie, was buried at Adath Jeshurun Cemetery on Grove Street in West Roxbury. Sixteen years later, Dunbar's widow, Gertrude, would be buried at Mount Pleasant Cemetery in Arlington, the town where she was born. The twice-married Dunbar remains in a single plot.

"Mr. Dunbar's landscapes grace the houses of many fanciers throughout the country," his obituary said.

A few days after Dunbar died, the *Cape Codder* newspaper eulogized him for his plans, way back in 1937, for the Cape to secede.

"He is survived by his wife Gertrude and a heritage of canvasses." A portion of that heritage was later found at and rescued from the town dump.

CHRISTOPHER RYDER HOUSE: 1953

In 1953, Donald and Louise Kastner bought an 1818 house on the corner of Orleans and Crows Pond Roads. The building had once served as a general store and post office and, until 1943, was owned by the Ryder family. In 1949, a tearoom had opened in the stately house, and now the Kastners had even bigger plans. They had the house lifted and turned ninety degrees so that it faced anyone driving north from the center of town. Soon they were able to seat 110 people for dinner. In 1962, they opened an opera house where many professional singers and actors got a start. After adding a Pavilion Room in 1968, they were able to seat 450 and featured singing waiters and waitresses.

"Most people could go out in the 1950s and '60s for an evening of fun," Kastner said. "They thoroughly enjoyed having dinner and going into the opera house for entertainment."[193]

In 1955, the Kastners staged a ball for fifty members of the Chatham Drama Guild. The Kastners themselves dressed as bartenders of the Gay Nineties. A "very charming vocal trio" called Three Angels—real estate man E. Melson Webster, school principal Richard Batchelder and Chester Hackett—were

The back bar at the Squire has become a repository of pieces of Chatham's history. Here is the original sign from the Christopher Ryder House restaurant. Note the bras hanging over the stained glass. *Photo by the author.*

costumed in "exquisite beaded gowns of the roaring twenties." Others dressed as devils, Catherine the Great, Hawaiian girls and gypsy girls.[194]

Masquerade dances were popular in the 1950s. The previous summer, Mr. and Mrs. Jack Keane had hosted a barbecue chicken masquerade party. Mrs. William Mayo won a prize for best costume: she came as a harem dancer. Mr. Keane himself, dressed as a swami, handed out cigarette lighters as party favors. "Movies were made during the barbeque for blackmail purposes—so look out," a newspaper columnist joked.[195]

"I Pray for Joe Every Night"

A few days before Hurricane Carol hit in August 1954, Senator Joe McCarthy's notorious sidekick Roy Cohn arrived in Brewster in a "supersized Cadillac" to address an overflow crowd of over five hundred people who came from all over the Cape. His topic: the Menace of Communism. Since 1951, a legislative committee under state Senator Philip G. Bowker had been investigating Communism in Massachusetts.[196]

The Army-McCarthy hearings had been broadcast on live TV earlier in the year, ending in June, and Cohn, who had graduated from Columbia Law School at age twenty and had played a key role in the 1951 espionage trial of Julius and Ethel Rosenberg, was a star. This was his first public appearance since the hearings.

"The boyish Cohn"—he was twenty-seven—"looked small and slight of stature. The brooding face and darting eyes picked up by the TV cameras were not in evidence."[197] Cohn wore a light gray summer suit, pants that needed pressing and black shoes.

"Pictures, words and music combined are coming soon out of the ether, for Cape Cod," the *Cape Codder* crowed in a 1948 front-page story about TV. This West Chatham family is shown in front of its TV in the mid-'50s. *Photo courtesy of the Chatham, Massachusetts Historical Society.*

In his speech, he traced the history of Communism, saying that twenty-five to thirty-five thousand Communists were operating in the United States. He ended by "warning his audience to watch for communist influence in the press and in the schools."

Afterward, a crowd, mainly of middle-aged women who called him "Roy," gathered for a half hour at the stage to ask Cohn to autograph scraps of paper. One woman blessed him and said she prayed for "Joe" every night.

About a week later, Hurricane Carol struck, causing extensive damage to boats in Pleasant Bay. "The Chatham waterfront took a beating as waters rose five feet above normal in many places, washed out roads and generally turned the normally peaceful aspect of Stage Harbor into a yachtsman's nightmare."[198] Champlain Road was awash with skiffs lining the roadside. The Chatham Post Office on the corner of Main Street and Chatham Bars Avenue lost a plate-glass window, and George Shole's Piper Cub at the airport lost its wing.

If that wasn't bad enough, a few days later Hurricane Edna swept through, causing low-lying parts of the southerly side of Chatham to be evacuated.

ALL THESE PEOPLE

Feet. Over the course of the summer of 1950, the feet of the thousands of summer visitors crossing Main Street to and from the post office had obliterated the crosswalks and other white lines. The lines needed to be painted twice a year, said Police Chief Benjamin F. Rollins.

Who did these feet belong to? Who knew? After World War II, "the vacation became democratized" as most workers now had a two-week vacation.[199] "Tourism had become the region's major industry by the early 1950s." In that period, while tourism brought in $70 million to the Cape, agriculture, fishing and manufacturing brought in a paltry $8 million.

In 1953, the town planning board recommended "the development of a secondary road, parallel to Main Street, for the purpose of relieving the flow of traffic on Main Street."

By the summer of 1954, the Main Street congestion problem had become so dire that the town tried something new: making Main Street one way from Old Harbor Road to Chatham Bars Avenue by the post office. Rollins believed that although some complained about Main Street being one way—merchants generally do not like a one-way street—it reduced congestion and relieved the parking problem. Moreover, there were no accidents, whereas the day the traffic reverted to two-way, several accidents occurred. Rollins strongly recommended that traffic remain one-way every summer from June 15 to September 15. His recommendation was not taken.

Up at the First National store, Cliff at the fish counter caused a ruckus showing off a six-inch bronze harpoon head found in the flesh of a swordfish. Cliff planned to mount the harpoon head over his own mantel.[200]

In September 1956, when the main post office moved much farther down Main Street to a building with parking, the commercial area was less congested.

"The new building will not see so many box patrons who found the old location ideal for a one-stop mail and shopping expedition," wrote Mildred R. Caldwell in her Chatham column in the *Cape Codder*.[201] Mail delivery had also been instituted all over town.

Finally, in about 1959, the town improved the busy intersection by the First Congregational Church, where Main Street meets Old Harbor and Stage Harbor Roads, by installing a rotary. The church, which had once been known as the Little Church on the Hill and then the Church of the Murals, now was often called the Church at the Rotary.

I KISS YOUR FAMOUS FEET

A host of well-known and distinguished people made Chatham a second home during the 1950s. One day, a young woman named Beatrice Beverly walked through the drowsy streets of North Chatham toward the old Hattie Baxter House.[202] The house was built in 1780 and was once run as a rooming house. Back in the days of the clipper ships, this part of Chatham had been the old town center. Eventually, the sands shifted, the old wharves silted over and the commerce moved elsewhere.

But on this day, Beatrice's thoughts were not on history. A famous Broadway personality lived in Baxter House, and Beatrice was nervous.

In the late 1930s or early 1940s, John Cecil Holm, then a forty-something actor and playwright originally from Philadelphia, bought Baxter House and renovated it. Holm was on a roll since his "hilarious" play *Three Men on a Horse* enjoyed a two-year, record-breaking run on Broadway. In 1936, the play, which followed the exploits of Erwin (pronounced by all "Oy-win"), was made into a film. Erwin, a writer of greeting cards, was discovered in a saloon by a trio of racetrack sharks who exploited his almost supernatural talent for picking winning horses.[203]

Holm and his wife, Faith, were friendly with Peter Hunt, the fashionable folk art painter and decorator based in Provincetown. Hunt worked on the dining room of the house, visually lowering the ceiling by putting a plate rail around it, creating a Dutch door for a closet and building shelves, bunks and storage. Hunt "did all the painting himself. He brought down workers from Provincetown" in 1939 or 1940.[204]

When Hunt wrote *Peter Hunt's Cape Cod Cookbook*, the Holms were the only Chatham residents important enough for Hunt, a compulsive name-dropper, to include. "Often we would drive through the summer evening to dine on their terrace under the arbors, usually with interesting guests—often the casts from the Dennis Players or the Monomoy Theatre," Hunt wrote.[205]

And what did Hunt, the Holms and the thespians eat on these magical evenings "overlooking the outer ocean"? Spaghetti with garlic bread. And the secret to Faith Holm's spaghetti sauce? Finely ground round steak and two drops of Tabasco sauce.

But on this occasion, Faith Holm was not busy in the kitchen with spaghetti sauce. She was, in fact, laid up with a broken foot. "My hostess was very quiet and gentle and put me at my ease. But my host John Cecil Holm, took my young breath away in his Lord and Taylor lounging outfit," Beatrice wrote.

Holm then escorted the young girl outdoors to admire some birdfeeders.

Faith Holm died in 1959, and the following year, Holm married Delores Boland. Perhaps living in her predecessor's house bothered the new Mrs. Holm; Holm sold the house completely furnished in 1961.[206]

The Broadway actress Shirley Booth had starred as a gangster's moll in the 1935 production of *Three Men on a Horse*, and now Miss Booth, too, lived part time in Chatham, around the corner from Holm. She often acted in play festivals at the Cape Playhouse in Dennis during the summers.[207]

People from the international political stage also made Chatham their home. General Lucius D. Clay, who administered Germany after World War II, and his wife, the former Marjorie McKeown, daughter of the president of the New England Button Company, lived in the new Harbor Coves estate. They had bought the 210-year-old house known as Square Top overlooking Crow's Pond from Harold and Mary Moye. Harold Moye would later make his mark as the developer of Chatham's largest subdivision, Riverbay. And not far from Clay lived the ambassador to Peru, Theodore Achilles, and his wife, Marian.[208]

THE OLD MILL GRINDS ON

"I can remember seeing the slats of the arms covered with canvas and the arms themselves revolving against the sky as I looked up at them," Joseph Lincoln wrote.[209] "I can remember the groaning of the shaft as it turned and, when we went inside, the squeaking and trembling of the whole structure."

Lincoln, who was born in 1870, was reminiscing about a working windmill that he visited in his childhood. In his 1935 essay, he ridicules the fact that the windmills one might see now on Cape Cod had been gentrified into "Mrs. Coles-Graham's little guest house." While he applauds the preservation of the windmills, he decries the loss of the world of which working mills were a part.

In 1707, Colonel Godfrey built a mill off Stage Harbor Road—one of the earliest of the eleven mills built in town. The three-story octagonal mill, which stood thirty feet high on a hill, was a boon to sailors who used it to guide them before the lighthouses were built.

The mill's second and third floors were used for grinding flour and meal. A unique feature of the mill is a corncob grinder on the ground floor. It is driven from a stone spindle by two cast-iron spur wheels.[210]

"I can remember seeing the slats of the arms covered with canvas and the arms themselves revolving against the sky as I looked up at them," novelist Joseph C. Lincoln wrote in *Cape Cod Yesterdays*. The Godfrey Mill was moved to Chase Park in 1954. *Photo courtesy of Gene Guild.*

Chatham's picturesque mill overlooked the Mill Pond. The mill creaked on until a severe storm in 1929 "tipped the head wrecking the trundle and arms." For the next twenty-five years, the mill grew more derelict. Eventually, its owner, Stuart Crocker, approached the selectmen saying that he would give the mill to the town if the town would move it off of his property on Stage Harbor Road. The selectmen agreed, and the mill was then moved to Chase Park. By 1954, the restored mill was used for grinding demonstrations and had a new life, not as a guesthouse, but as a tourist attraction.[211]

In 1956, Alice Walker Guild sat down again at her typewriter and wrote a fourteen-page pamphlet *Growing Food and The Story of the Old Mill*, which was sold at the Godfrey mill that year.[212]

THE ANTITHESIS OF A '50S SUBDIVISION

A walker on a woodsy North Chatham hillside off Whidah Road might be surprised to stumble upon two cannons of indeterminate age aimed roughly at Fox Hill in Bassing Harbor.

The cannons are yoked together by a brick and cement bench. The cannons, believed to have come from an eighteenth-century shipwreck, were placed here in 1904 by William H. Wentworth Jr., who once owned all of this land. Wentworth's family home, Sedge Holm, still stands on the shore overlooking Bassing Harbor not far from the cannons. Many years later, the rumor circulated that the cannons came from the pirate ship *Whydah*—no doubt a fanciful story. (The ship did lend its name to nearby Whidah Road, however.)[213]

The land that Wentworth bought was largely bare. "The scrub pine mixed with oak that now blankets many parts of the Cape was almost non-existent."

In the 1950s, Wentworth's daughter Dorothea Smith, who had inherited the land, honed her vision of how she would like the land to be subdivided for generations to come.

"It would be the antithesis of a 1950s style subdivision," John Yacobian writes. "The character of Cannon Hill, with its curved roads, common space, spacious one-acre lots, and first bylaws, was not happenstance. It was the intent of Dorothea Smith to create a planned community." Large trees could not be cut down without the association's permission; houses had to conform to architectural standards and had to be sited with certain setbacks. Utility wires were buried underground. In 1959, the Chatham

Planning Board approved the preliminary plat plan, which called for thirty-nine lots.

Smith also preserved Fox Hill by giving it to the Chatham Conservation Foundation.

Around the bend in the shoreline toward Chatham Port, the rumble of bulldozers again broke the silence. Three entrepreneurs known as B.C.W. Trust bought twenty-six acres of land to the east of Eastward, Ho! Country Club for $70,000. The twenty-six acres "surrounded a beautiful 6-acres freshwater pond" called Fox Pond, just fifty yards from Pleasant Bay and seventy-five yards from Crow's Pond. "It was virtually a game preserve and a bird sanctuary all rolled into one." The developers called the new subdivision Fox Run, "whacked the land up into 20 building lots and sold them at figures to show a probable gross profit of over $500,000."[214]

Fox Run would soon adjoin the Eastward Point subdivision, which was begun in the early 1960s on the site of the old World War I Naval Air Station.

The subdivisions brought people who needed town services. The birthrate, too, had been rising since the war, with a high of seventy-one births in 1956. In September of that same year, Chatham's new primary school, which cost $375,000, opened with over two hundred pupils. "Class rooms are equipped with drinking fountains and wash bowls, and with alcove coat rooms with sliding doors." One wall of each room was all windows.[215]

RUMBLINGS OF A SEASHORE

Private Beach. No Trespassing. No Picnickers.

Everything came with a price. While the building boom brought many new jobs to Chatham, the population growth also destroyed the vestiges of an unfettered Eden.

With unprecedented growth came a realization that the swimming holes that everyone was used to visiting without a care in the world were suddenly private property. Dana Eldridge and his friends went to swim in Goose Pond one evening after the war only to find Keep Out signs posted. "Change, not all of it welcome, was on the way, and we would have to get used to it."[216]

Before the influx of people, everyone took access to the beaches for granted. When hotels, residential resort colonies and wealthy property owners bought shore land, public access was curtailed, and "the need to preserve beaches for general public use became evident."[217]

Interest in the national parks had been growing since Roosevelt's Works Progress Administration focused on them during the Depression. On November 1, 1956, *Cape Codder* editor Malcolm Hobbs broke the story that, based on its 1955 survey, the National Park Service was going ahead with plans for a Cape Cod National Seashore that would encompass parts of the coastline in Chatham, Orleans, Eastham, Wellfleet, Truro and Provincetown. It was becoming clear that if places were not set aside and protected, houses would soon line even the beaches.

By early 1959, as plans moved ahead for a national seashore, the lines were literally drawn in the sand as Chatham vigorously protested, through the mouth of Selectman Robert McNeece, the inclusion of Morris and Stage Islands, Hardings Beach and Monomoy in the seashore.[218] McNeece apparently called in his chits on influential Chatham summer residents who had close ties in Washington, D.C.[219]

In contrast, Alice Hiscock, chair of the Chatham Planning Board, favored the islands' inclusion in the seashore, and she spoke about the subdivisions that were planned by the owners of Morris and Stage Islands. Ultimately, those four parts of Chatham were subtracted from what is, in the twenty-first century, the over forty-three thousand acres of the Cape Cod National Seashore.

In 1958, when the $425,000 Morris Island causeway connected the island to the mainland, lots became even more attractive. Soon, the planning board accepted thirty-six lots on 213-acre Morris Island and an additional thirty-eight lots on Stage Island.

A STRANGE KIND OF DEATH

Shore Road, which runs for about a mile along the town's easternmost coast, is one of Chatham's most exclusive addresses. It is here that the Chatham Bars Inn was built in 1914 with a breathtaking view of the Atlantic. And it was here that Joseph Lincoln built his own house, Crosstrees, a couple of years later.

The final summer of the decade was over now, and it was the time of year when "conversations turn to talk of cranberries, bayberries and beach plum jelly, to hats and fall clothes."[220]

It was midmorning on Wednesday, September 23, when a local doctor and an ambulance were summoned to a twelve-room house on the water view side of Shore Road. A summer resident who had returned to town had somehow been stabbed in the abdomen. Medical help was needed.[221]

The man was Walter F. Munford, the fifty-nine-year-old head of U.S. Steel Corporation. A local doctor had been treating Munford for several months for "fatigue" and "nervous exhaustion." Now, Munford was bleeding from the waist.

As the story trickled out in the newspapers over the next several days, a strange and improbable series of details came to light.

Since the day after he took over U.S. Steel the previous May, Munford had been engaged in difficult negotiations with United Steelworkers of America. Eventually, President Eisenhower stepped in to meet with the unions.

On this particular Wednesday morning, Robert B. O'Connor, U.S. Steel's house physician, and the company's vice-president, Harvey M. Jordan, had both been overnight guests of Munford and his wife, Camille, in the Shore Road house. Apparently, O'Connor had recommended that Munford travel to Boston for further treatment for his nervous condition, and Munford was due to leave later in the day.

The tale as it emerged was this: The four had sat down to a late breakfast, and a little after 10:00 a.m. they were clearing the dining room table and carrying the dirty dishes into the kitchen, which was up a little step from the dining room. Camille walked into the kitchen to find her husband bleeding from the waist and gripping a five-inch fish knife in his hand. Camille later told District Attorney Edmund Dinis, who ordered an investigation, that she believed her husband had slipped on the "highly polished" flagstone floor and cut himself open when he fell directly onto the knife.

Shortly after noon, a surgeon at Cape Cod Hospital repaired the three-inch gash in Munford's abdomen. The hospital issued a statement that the knife had missed Munford's heart.

The prominence of the man involved coupled with the bizarre nature of the knife wound put the Munford story in national and local headlines for a week. State police were investigating; Dinis wanted to know if the wounds were self-inflicted or "otherwise."

The story turned again when, after initially rallying, Munford suffered a cerebral thrombosis the day after his surgery. Dinis, meanwhile, announced that he found no evidence of "any criminal assault," "wrongdoing" or "that the wound was self inflicted." It was an accident, Dinis said, something that occurred while putting away utensils.

Three days later, Munford was eased into an oxygen tent; Camille and their sons, Robert and Walter, held vigil at his bedside. On September 28, five days after the stabbing, Munford died. He was buried at Union Cemetery.

"I think he was worn out by the long steel strike," a neighbor said. "We will miss him."[222]

THE END OF AN ERA

A few days later, Chatham lost a bit of its living history. Peter Zaimes, a Greek immigrant, moved away to live with his cousins in Lynn. Zaimes had arrived in Chatham in 1914 and worked the sandy streets as a horse-and-wagon peddler of fruits and vegetables. In 1928, he and his partner, Louis Zianos, bought land on Main Street and built the Epicure Building. The front of the store had two doors—as it does to this day. Through one door was Chatham's first restaurant, the Chatham Café, and through the other was a grocery store affiliated with S.S. Pierce.[223]

Ill health had forced Zaimes to retire, and he lived quietly on Doane Road across the street from the house he had shared with Zianos until Zianos's death. In retirement, Zaimes tended his gardens and charmed his neighbors with his Greek cooking. In the weeks before he moved, "friends have been driving him about Chatham showing him the new developments which he compared to the Chatham he knew forty-five years ago."

Without doubt, Chatham had changed tremendously. And it would continue to change in the 1960s.

The Age of Aquarius

When the moon is in the Seventh House
And Jupiter aligns with Mars
Then peace will guide the planets
And love will steer the stars
This is the dawning of the age of Aquarius.
—Galt MacDermot, Hair

SOME REALLY, REALLY GOOD FRIES

The squawking of seagulls. The glint of sunlight on water. The sea breeze. The cool air first struck young Fred Byrne when he and his sisters stepped out of the family car after the sticky eight-hour drive from New York. A flat tire always made grueling the slow miles east through Providence and the little towns that followed along Route 6.[224]

"I always remember the air was so different," Fred says. Back home in Westchester in July and August, the air hung heavy with humidity. In Chatham, at his grandmother's cottage where the family would spend an entire month, "it hits you. It's cooler. You get the sea breeze. It's like a breath of fresh air."

Fred's grandmother, Mary Byrne, owned seven acres on the corner of Bridge Street and Stage Harbor Road. There, in 1954, she built a cottage where the families of her sons, Fred and Steven, traded off July and August. Sometimes Fred's family spent a second month nearby in the Horne Cottages on Morris Island Road below the lighthouse.

Fred's uncle Bob, who married late, made his home with Fred's grandmother in the 1960s. During Mary's afternoon bridge parties, Bob, "a sharp dresser," would serve the ladies glasses of Dubonnet. Alice Stallknecht, now a widow living alone a few houses away on Stage Harbor Road, was a regular.

For Fred, an idyllic summer day meant sailing. Chatham yacht designer and builder F. Spaulding Dunbar had designed a class of wooden Catabouts for the Stage Harbor Yacht Club, and the Byrne family owned one.

"We really had the life of Riley," Fred recalls about his teenage years. "We played on the water all day. It was like the best of all worlds."

Mary Byrne first came to Chatham in the early 1940s with her husband, Frederick. Frederick was an electrical engineer in Westchester County, and after a few summers with their three sons in Falmouth, Mary discovered Chatham. They moved an antique double Cape house from Route 28 in West Chatham to a hill on their lot that overlooked the Mill Pond.[225] The couple then hired a local contractor to restore the house; they also landscaped the grounds. Frederick died before he was able to enjoy it.

The house "was very New England style," Fred recalls. "The kitchen was very plain."

During the war summers, while Fred's father and his two uncles served in the U.S. Navy, Fred's mother, Becky, shared the Chatham house with her mother-in-law and her two baby girls. By the '60s, though, Fred's usual summer companions were his parents and the three younger of his five sisters.

The Byrne children quickly made friends at the Stage Harbor Yacht Club, just up the road from the house, and Fred fell in with a group his own age. All day long, Fred's parents "just let me run," he recalls. "They knew that food was my biggest thing and I would show up to sit down for dinner."

Rick Smith, one of four children of the Reverend Carlyle Smith and his wife, Janet, was a year younger than Fred and also learning to sail at the yacht club. The Reverend Smith had come from western Massachusetts to take over the pulpit of the First Congregational Church in August 1958. The family moved into the church parsonage on Seaview Street, overlooking Sears Park.

After a morning on the water, the sailing students would dock and walk over to a clam shack on Bridge Street. Shoestring French fries—a precursor to McDonald's thin fries—were the attraction. "French fries for a quarter," Rick Smith recalls.

"They tasted like clams because they never changed their oil," Fred adds. "Everything there tasted like clams."

The screens in the windows of the small dining room into which tourists occasionally lapsed were covered with grease. Fred and Rick loved the place.

A PRESIDENTIAL RETREAT

In November 1960, the election of John F. Kennedy to the White House put Cape Cod on the national map. As iconic photos of JFK sailing on the *Honey Fitz* in Nantucket Sound appeared in the news, more and more people wanted to see the place where it was happening. The Kennedy compound in Hyannis Port was about twenty-five miles west from Chatham along Route 28.

And why not go to Cape Cod? The Kennedys were an attractive young couple, and the Cape seemed an appealing place. And once on the Cape, why not drive down to the elbow and take a peek at Chatham? While in the past every visitor would have gone first to the overlook at Chatham Light, now visitors could see a new tourist attraction growing every year in popularity to rival the lighthouse: the fish pier.

Remodeled and updated during World War II, the fish pier on Shore Road, about a mile north of the Chatham Light, was luring so many tourists that parking was difficult. It is hard to describe the strange attraction that viewing a homely fishing boat pulling into a wharf held for the city folk. Perhaps fishing represented a fantasy life for many of these professional people and office workers down from Boston.

Barbara Aaronson with the author at the Chatham Fish Pier in August 1966. Almost as soon as it opened in 1946, the fish pier joined the Chatham Light as a major draw for tourists. *Photo courtesy of the author.*

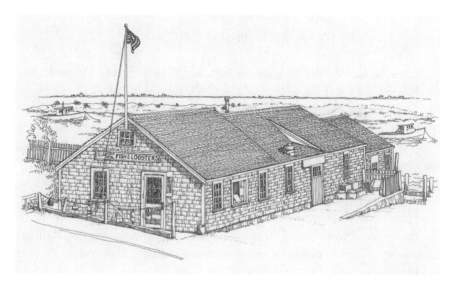

World War II veteran Willard Nickerson and his wife, Frances, opened Nickerson's Fish and Lobsters next to the fish pier in 1950. Clean salt water was piped through to keep the quahogs fresh. *Original pen-and-ink drawing courtesy of artist Kassie Foss.*

Another draw was certainly Nickerson's Fish and Lobsters, established by Willard Nickerson in 1950. The business, although no longer run by the Nickerson family, is in operation to this day.

In the 1960 *Report of the Town Officers*, the wharfinger noted the jump in the number of "spectators and visitors who came to see the daily fish catch unloaded and packed for market." In 1963, the wharfinger again noted that the number of visitors was increasing. In 1964, things were hopping so much at the fish pier that he sent someone out to tabulate the visitors on two afternoons in July. And how many people came? On the first afternoon, 1,073; and on the second, 1,159.

"This tends to show, along with the fishing industry, the bearing that the Town Pier has on the economy of the Town in general," he concluded.

"The vacation market, which had been more exclusive and sophisticated before the war, expanded tremendously," wrote one Cape Cod observer.[226] "Much of the mass market, led by baby boom families, was not as interested in the subtleties of horticulture, architecture, or folklore as in the basic beach vacation. The overarching appeal of the Cape became the sun, sand, and surf."

In 1962, when Ursula Andress stepped out of the surf in *Dr. No* wearing a white bikini, the beach became a much sexier place. The 1950s bathing suits with corsets, zipper and bra cups gave way to the bikini and to less-structured one-piece suits. Hugh Hefner slapped a model in a bikini on the cover of a 1962 *Playboy*; *Sports Illustrated* published its first swimsuit issue in 1964.

Chatham's perpetual lure was its pristine Nantucket Sound Beaches: Harding, Ridgevale, Cockle Cove, Forest, Pleasant Street. You could also swim below the lighthouse, in Pleasant Bay, in the Oyster Pond and in the Mill Pond. It was a town of beaches for any taste, where bikinis, sand, surf and sun all rolled into one sexy place to cultivate a really good tan.

HIGHWAYS AND BYWAYS

By 1959, the Mid-Cape Highway had been completed, and in 1963, Route 3 from Boston was also completed. The stage was now set for a mass exodus from Boston during the hot summer months. It was easier than ever to travel to Cape Cod.

"Americans of the 1950s and 1960s were in love with the road. This was a boom time for motels," observed one historian.[227] "Motels were the perfect partner to the automobile in democratizing leisure travel during the 1950s and 1960s." In Chatham, new motels dotted Route 28 between Main Street and the Harwich line.

In 1960, the eleven police officers and nineteen special police officers serving under Chief Rollins drove 93,842.6 miles without ever leaving Chatham.

THE LITTLE CHURCH ON THE HILL GROWS UP

Summer visitors tend to think that Chatham hibernates from September to June. But a few days after Kennedy's election, on November 20, a groundbreaking ceremony was held for a new parish house at the First Congregational Church.

The church building, erected in 1830 in what is now Union Cemetery, had been remodeled and moved to its new location about a mile north in 1866.

By the late 1950s, the boxy church had become too small for the needs of a modern congregation. The two-story addition would provide offices for the minister, the secretary and other staff, as well as rooms for the Sunday school and restrooms. The church borrowed $45,000 to erect the new

Before the First Congregational Church had an electronic carillon, boys had to climb into the belfry every Sunday to ring the bells. Here, Rick Smith (left) and his brother, Jackson, sons of the Reverend Carlyle Smith, ring the bell circa 1959. *Photo courtesy of Rick Smith.*

wing.[228] Construction of the addition moved along well, allowing the wing to be dedicated on June 25.

For many years, ministers had shuffled through the church at a rate that must have necessitated an almost permanent search committee. In the ten years since the war ended, the church had had five ministers. Under the sway of the Reverend Carlyle Smith's charismatic personality, the church prospered and grew. In 1962, 500 people attended the church on Easter Sunday. The church grew from fewer than 100 members to over 300; during the summer, Smith preached to two full services. A youth director, John Button, was brought in to lead the Sunday school, which had an enrollment of over 125.

Smith was in his forties when he arrived, and "he really brought the community together. He was young enough to rally around the parents and kids," his son Rick remembers.

On October 25, 1964, during an afternoon service overseen by eleven other ministers in the Barnstable Association of Congregational Christian Churches, Carlyle Smith was ordained before a packed church.

The Reverend Carlyle Smith at a groundbreaking for the new wing of the First Congregational Church of Chatham. Smith, who served as pastor in the 1960s, spearheaded the movement to expand the cramped church. *Photo courtesy of Rick Smith.*

The moderator asked Smith, "Do you engage to tend the flock of God that is your charge?" and Smith responded, "I do so engage, God being my helper."[229]

"I have never met another clergyman who is loved more by his colleagues in the ministry," the Reverend Stephen W. Brown of East Dennis wrote about Smith in July 1966. "He possesses a depth of spiritual life that I have rarely seen in others."

FROM MOON HOUSE TO DUNE HOUSE

Gertrude Wright, the widow of Richardson Wright and his coauthor on the *Cape Codder* column "Chatham on the Half Shell," decided to move after the death of her husband in 1961.

Gertrude was Richardson's third wife, and at the time of their courtship, he had been known as "one of New York City's most eligible bachelors," despite—or because of—his "strong physical resemblance to Adolph Hitler."[230] Gertrude and Richardson had moved to Moon House at the end of Barn Hill Road when Richardson retired from his long career editing *House & Garden*. There the pair gardened, befriended their neighbors, planned European travels and wrote. Now that Richardson was gone, Gertrude did not plan to go far.

Just around the corner from Moon House, Gertrude built Dune House in a development called Harding Shores. Early in 1950, developers bulldozed a sandy bluff of pitch pines to flatten it out. By March 30, plats had been certified. The first modest houses built there were dubbed "tacky," even though they were created from stock plans by Boston architect Royal Barry Wills, who was known in mid-century for breathing life into the traditional Cape Cod house style.

During the summer of 1960, as ground was broken for five homes in Harding Shores, the Harding Shores Association was formed in the living room of resident Doug Williams. Annual dues were twenty-five dollars; an opening and closing season cocktail party soon became a tradition in this summer community.

In a more permanent way than the summer colonies, which were small enclaves of cottages catering to a transient summer population, Harding Shores grew to be a familiar family enclave. Rudy Czufin from St. Louis was known as the "mayor of Harding Shores." He and his wife, Dot, were a gregarious pair who welcomed newcomers, introduced people to one another and gave out small welcome gifts.

OH, SANTA MARIA!

Radio Station Chatham was again in the national news early in 1961 when pirates captured the Portuguese liner the *Santa Maria* in the South Atlantic. After the ship disappeared into radio silence, it suddenly sent a message shortly after midnight on January 24, when the *Santa Maria*'s operator contacted Wireless Cape Cod (WCC). In all, a total of 111 messages were exchanged.

"This last week was the most frantic in the station's long history, although operators here at one time or another have been the sole contact with ships, planes or explorers' camps that were in the eyes of the world," read a *New York Herald Tribune* article on February 10, 1961.

The article rehashed the station's glory days when it exchanged messages with the Byrd Expedition to the South Pole, Anne and Charles Lindbergh in 1932 and Howard Hughes in 1938. Operator Francis Doane talked to the dirigible *Hindenburg* a few seconds before it exploded over Lakehurst, New Jersey, in 1937.

"For all its import as a funnel of news, Chatham Radio is not much more distinguished looking than the cranberry bog" that was nearby, the reporter concluded.

THE DADDY OF THEM ALL: RIVERBAY

For some time, Chatham had been attracting prominent people from the Boston area. In 1945, businessman Harold Moye bought the house Square Top overlooking Crow's Pond. Harold had been vacationing on Cape Cod with his wife, Mary, and their son, Jack, since the 1940s. During the off-season, he was a Chevrolet dealer in Quincy and, later, also in Newton.[231]

A friend of Moye owned a nightclub in Weymouth, as well as a hunting lodge in Harwich. His friend wanted to develop the Harwich land but didn't know how to go about it. Moye ultimately bought one hundred acres of the land and, with investors from the Quincy Shipyards, developed it into the Great Sand Lakes development. The finest model house, with three bedrooms, sold for $12,900, Jack recalls.

In the late 1950s, Moye bought three hundred acres in Chatham for about $300,000 and then spent "umpteen millions" developing the fifteen winding roads in what would be called Riverbay Estates. This giant parcel

Riverbay Estates, developed by Harold Moye in the early 1960s, remains the largest subdivision in Chatham with about 338 homes. An ad for Haromar Homes advertised "features most wanted by today's home buyer." *Photo by the author.*

overlooked the Monomoy River, and the most desirable lots were on the bluff above the river. (Moye later gave the ribbon of riverfront land to the Conservation Commission.)

Jack had married Bess in 1951, and after a stint in the Coast Guard, Jack took over a Chevrolet dealership in Hyannis. The young family moved first to West Dennis and then, in 1960, to a house overlooking Nantucket Sound in South Chatham. Sea Change, which they occupied for a year, was built in 1938 by the poet John Peale Bishop, a classmate of F. Scott Fitzgerald's at Princeton. From that house, the growing family moved to Hiawatha, a square top on Cross Street. There the Moyes raised their five children.

Meanwhile, the 401 building lots of Riverbay were laid out. When building began, the new owners could choose from a prototype design or bring in their own designs, subject to approval by Moye, who encouraged the use of local builders, Jack remembers.

The ads for Riverbay were geared, in the early 1960s, to the retirement set. In a monthly supplement to the *Cape Codder* called "Riverbay Review," ads showed two duffers with a golf cart outside their home. "The Executive," a four-bed, three-bath home with an incinerator, was offered at $28,000.

TIME MARCHES ON

Oh, come ye home to Chatham Town,
All who have wandered far...
Come home and help us celebrate,
One and all—wherever you are!
— *Harriet E. Tuttle, poem commemorating Chatham's 250th anniversary*

What primitive urge fuels our love of burying time capsules? Does a time capsule speak to a desire to stop time, or does it speak more to the burial of the dead? Back in 1924, when the cornerstone for Main Street School was laid, town officials watched as a tin box containing a copy of the 1923 town annual report; the *Chatham Monitor* of May 20, 1924; the 200th anniversary book; and William Smith's *History of Chatham, Massachusetts* was buried.

In June 1962, residents celebrated the town's 250th anniversary by creating another time capsule containing letters and documents. Presumably, the capsule was to have been buried, "but no one ever got around to doing that," says Spencer Grey, a member of the town's tercentennial committee. "It sits in a vault at the town hall and I assume it will be opened on schedule."

The Age of Aquarius

Residents celebrated the town's 250th anniversary with great fanfare in 1962. Harold Tuttle (left) and Chester Eldredge display a time capsule containing letters and documents. Selectmen are to open the capsule, locked in a vault in town hall, on June 11, 2012. *Photo courtesy of the Chatham, Massachusetts Historical Society.*

The schedule set in 1962 calls for the selectmen to open the capsule on June 11, 2012. In 2012, Chatham will have a chance to brush up its image and present it to the world, just as it did in 1962 and 1912.

Pen-and-ink drawings of three sites were the icons used on stationery of Chatham's 250th anniversary committee. The town took as its totems the Old Mill (now a historic site), the 1752 Atwood House (now a museum) and the railroad station (now a museum). In 1912, these three places were still being used for their original purposes.

As events accelerated in the twentieth century, the past took a shorter time to become mummified. The Chatham Railroad Museum was created in a train station built seventy-five years previously when the railroad spur finally reached Chatham. The station fell into disuse in 1937 when the New York, New Haven & Hartford Railroad Company discovered that even the freight train that chugged into Chatham—passenger service had been discontinued some time before—was no longer viable.

The station was built in 1887 in the Railroad Gothic style. "The tower, with its candle snifter roof, is a fine balance to the boxy building and adds the bit of drama that is very welcome," a local architectural historian has written.[232]

In 1951, Chatham summer resident Phyllis Cox of Cleveland, Ohio, bought and restored the station and then gave it to the town. In July 1960, it opened as a new tourist attraction, housing over five hundred models, documents, photographs and objects, including more than seventy-nine hundred photographs of railroads, in a collection that was only in its infancy. That summer, 2,213 persons from twenty-nine states and four foreign countries visited the exhibit.

In 1953, Chatham native Avis Augusta Morton Chase gave land on Cross Street for a park named in honor of her late husband. The Old Godfrey Mill was given to the town by Stuart Miller Crocker and moved to Chase Park in 1954. Restored, the mill, like the railroad station and Chase Park itself, became new tourist attractions. In 1963, seventy-eight hundred visitors tramped through the park to the mill.

In 1962, Chatham's year-round population had topped thirty-three hundred; the number tripled in the summer. "Many retired people are choosing Chatham as a place to live and enjoy their retirement," the 250th commemorative pamphlet crowed. "Younger people are finding it a fine place to raise a family."

An air show on Sunday, August 5, would be a highlight of the weekend events. One of the stunts the "famous" Cole brothers would perform would be a "car to plane transfer." A photo showed what looks like a Buick convertible with a man on a ladder swinging from a small airplane dangling over its trunk. The Chatham Band would play before the show and during intermission. Sometime in August (to be announced), the lord mayor of Chatham, England, would have his day in town.

The pamphlet offers a snapshot of the town the way it was in 1962. Four doctors were practicing in town—Bradford Brown, E. Robert Harned, Henry Hopkins and, nearing the end of his practice, Doc Keene. The town had two dentists and an orthodontist. It had an optometrist and an osteopathic physician, Ruth W. Brown.

The cottage colonies were still prospering. An ad for the Horne Cottages on Morris Island Road advertises a marina, a putting green and softball, croquet and tennis facilities scattered among the cottages on the waterfront.

Many of those businesses taking out ads are still going strong today: the Mayflower Shop; Larry's PX; Pate's Charcoal Pit restaurant on Main Street; Eldredge & Lumpkin Insurance Agency; Pleasant Bay Village Motel; the Puritan; the Wayside Inn; and Chatham Jewelers, to name a few. Other businesses such as the Swinging Basket; Camp Avalon for Girls; Chatham Bowling Center; Bearse's Grocery Store; and Sign of the Blue Swan have entered the realm of nostalgia.

Baby Boomers Grow Up

As the baby boom generation progressed through the school system, the schools became crowded. The need for a new high school had grown acute as the red brick building on Main Street, built in 1924, became obsolete. By 1960 the school was so crowded that music classes were held in a "narrow locker room." In 1963, the town opened a new high school on Crowell Road. "The exterior of white clapboard and natural white cedar with its colonial appearance might be likened to a jewel, a gem with Chatham as its setting," the 1963 *Report of the Town Officers* rhapsodized. The building offered a "harmony of color" and—a hint that the visitor toured the school on a weekend—"a feeling of peace and quiet."

On November 10, the Reverend Alfred H. Tracy baptized sixteen persons, "the largest number ever baptized during his eleven years in the ministry and it is believed to be the largest number baptized at one time at the church." A newspaper photo shows parents, babies and children clustered in the front of the Methodist church, under the organ's pipes.[233]

Two weeks later, thirteen-year-old Ginny Nickerson was sitting in her eighth-grade music class in the Main Street School. It was just after lunch on November 22, 1963. Things were winding down this Friday afternoon six days before Thanksgiving. The auditorium was dim when someone entered the room and murmured to the teacher. The teacher turned to the class and perhaps paused for a moment before saying, "President Kennedy has been shot. The president is dead."

One girl began crying, Ginny remembers. "It seems as though everything just kind of stopped."

Rick Smith, who was ten, remembers an announcement blaring over the school public address system. "Everyone was just stunned."

Through the weekend, "Cape Cod quietly mourned the shocking death of John F. Kennedy, a man of Cape Cod, the nation and the world." Monday was a cold and blustery day, with bright sunshine, and the flags hung limp at half-mast. Everything was closed except for essential services such as gas stations and pharmacies. The three television networks broadcast the funeral. Rick remembers sitting in front of his family's black-and-white television watching it.

"Why is the sense of loss so great?" asked an editorial writer. "Why does it curl the heart with a pain that will not be quenched?"[234]

MORE WAS LOST

Every generation, at some point, looks around and notices something that has been lost. Now it was houses—the town's architectural heritage.

Cape Cod, Greek revival, Gothic revival, Italianate, Tuscan villas, Second Empire, Richardson Romanesque, Shingle style, Bungalow—take a look around Chatham and you'll see all of these styles dating from 1750 to the early twentieth century.[235]

As the 1964 *Report of the Town Officers* put it, events "focused a clear light on the need to find ways to honor and preserve [Chatham's] visible heritage." While the report commended the work of the Chatham Historical Society and of the Nickerson Society, it wanted to go further in saving the town's old houses.

"Before it is too late, and the bulldozer, 'progress' or 'remodeling' have destroyed the image which many cherish," legislation, in the form of historic districts, was needed to halt the demolition, the report said.

In 1963, the town appointed a six-member historical district study commission and, in 1965, an architectural advisory committee. Since

In the 1950s, as subdivisions began to overrun the town, interest grew in preserving Chatham's distinctive old houses. Today, anyone wishing to demolish an old house must appear before a town board. This saltbox dates probably from the Civil War. *Photo by the author.*

World War II, interest in preservation and restoration had increased nationwide. In 1957, on Nantucket Island, Walter Beinecke, an heir to the S&H Green Stamp fortune, bought up the old, deteriorating waterfront and refurbished it. In an article in *Time* magazine on July 26, 1968, Beinecke invoked the old specter of the hot dog in describing the kind of visitor he wanted the new Nantucket to attract. "Instead of selling six postcards and two hot dogs you have to sell a hotel room and a couple of sports coats."

In Chatham, the commission noted, landmark buildings gave the town a "distinctive image" and "represent a part of the local history which should be kept as a bridge between the past and future. Preservation is possible without impairing healthy growth of a Town and may even assist such growth."

In 1962, a new conservation movement kicked off with the founding of the Chatham Conservation Foundation. "The record, written all over the Cape in the form of cut-over woodland and wasted topsoil, does not say much for human foresight at any time, with or without the bulldozers," the conservation writer John Hay noted in 1963.[236]

The Dream of Monomoy

The eight-mile sand spit known as Monomoy is "as eerie, isolated, gleaming a bar as ever shone back at the moon," Elizabeth Reynard wrote in 1934 in *The Narrow Land*.[237]

Folklore has it that a mooncusser attached two lanterns to his old white horse and made him tramp the sands of Monomoy, luring in ships that mistook the horse's lights for a safe harbor. During the night of a wild gale, the man mounted the horse. When the horse swam out to sea, the mooncusser drowned. But the white stallion is still out there "and when the moon comes out may be seen close to the pointed prows of ships, his white mane gleaming as he guides them over the bars."

Something about the image of the white stallion swimming in the sea—elusive, always out of touch, yet beneficent—suggests a metaphor for Monomoy itself, where "the sands lie, an unbroken expanse, on the long sea spit."

Monomoy is a barrier island resting on a bed of glacial material left eighteen thousand years ago when the great glaciers retreated. Monomoy is younger than the Cape, perhaps eight thousand years old, and was used by Native Americans for fishing and hunting.[238] French and English explorers

"There is nothing left except the beauty and the serenity of perhaps the most beautiful single place I ever been on this earth," wrote a lover of Monomoy after it became a national wilderness area in 1970. *Photo by William Camiré. Copyright William Camiré.*

mapping the coast in the sixteenth century called it Cape Malabar—the Cape of Evil Bars.

"The winter fires of Monomoy burn with strange hues from black wreck-wood seasoned in many climes." So a writer noted in a February 1865 article in *Harper's New Monthly*.

In the early nineteenth century, residents were so confident of Monomoy's fidelity that they deigned to create a year-round village called Whitewash around Powder Hole, a deep natural harbor. Whitewash had about two hundred residents—most engaged in fishing—a tavern inn and a public school. But by 1860, Monomoy had betrayed them, as it ultimately betrays anyone who takes it for granted. A hurricane in 1860 shifted the sands.

Yet a fever burns in those who love Monomoy. For those who knew it in youth, it remains the gold standard of beauty. "We went barefoot and at the beginning of each summer my feet were tender. But soon they toughened and even sharp beach grass gave me no problem," Harry D. Ellis recalled of his childhood summers on Monomoy during the final decade of the nineteenth century. "I recall that in our wanderings, I found patches of wild sweet peas and a little patch of pink morning glories. I enjoyed bringing these flowers home to my mother at Sunset Cottage, where she put them in a jelly glass on the kitchen windowsill."

How primal are Ellis's recollections, evoking as they do the innocence of boyhood, the love of nature and of a mother. He brought morning glories home to Sunset Cottage, and there was mother, ready with a jelly glass, in the kitchen. Nothing is discordant. And yet it is all but a memory by the time Ellis speaks of it, when he is ninety and living in a radically changed world.

"Monomoy, from Hardings Beach, always looked like it had a halo around it," Dana Eldridge wrote in his memoir *Cape Cod Lucky*.

By the 1930s, families were driving to Monomoy in "woodies," automobiles with wooden sides and oversized balloon tires, from which the air was released to make driving in the sand easier. A Monomoy culture had been built up around fishing, hunting, camping and drinking. The decommissioned lighthouse, now in private hands, became a gathering spot.

In late July 1940, eleven-year-old Peter Hartley teased the men at the Morris Island Coast Guard Station into bringing him for a few days' trip to the Monomoy Point Station, built in 1902. Hartley spent hours in the Monomoy station's tower, watching the ships pass by through powerful binoculars. "And in those days, too, the last remnants of the great days of coastal sail, the broken-backed, warped three-masted schooners were still plying their lumber and granite trade between Maine, the Maritimes and New York and the south, and carrying coal back north."[239]

Weirdly, Hartley also saw, spread around Powder Hole, thirty or forty "camps"—shacks, really—some dating to the mid-nineteenth century. Living on the cheap in these camps were mainly women and children; at the tail end of the Depression, the men of the families were elsewhere working or looking for work. The Coast Guard truck picked up groceries and provisions for them at the First National on its daily trip back to town.

Just after the war, Coast Guard coxswain Bernie Webber, who would later gain fame for leading the heroic rescue of men from the *Pendleton*, was stationed at the Monomoy Point Station. Alone there, "one would swear that he heard voices and footsteps, thinking perhaps they came from the ghosts of old surfmen that had served at Monomoy long ago."[240]

Yet Monomoy's days as a place for the living were numbered as the federal "taking" by eminent domain drew closer.

The first move, innocent on the face of it, came in 1929, when the federal government passed the Migratory Bird Act. The following year, the government fixed its eye on Monomoy as a bird preserve.

In 1942, Selectman Edwin F. Eldredge begged for a delay. "The people of Cape Cod are giving up from their lives loved ones, buying bonds until it hurts, giving time to civilian defense programs," he was quoted as saying.

"For the federal government to establish at a great cost bird sanctuaries, not only on Cape Cod, but all over the United States, is an unpatriotic gesture in these times."

One can almost hear Eldredge spit the words "bird sanctuary." Yet in 1944, the federal government took Monomoy and declared it a National Wildlife Refuge. Oddly enough, despite the government's often-expressed concern for birdlife, the military repeatedly bombed and strafed Monomoy in aerial practice missions that began during World War II and continued through 1949.

If that wasn't bad enough, in the 1950s the original proposal for the Cape Cod National Seashore included Monomoy. After the town fought that off, something else cropped up: Congress wanted to declare Monomoy a wilderness area. This would mean that the use of Monomoy would be further curtailed and policed. In April 1958, the sands of Monomoy shifted again. Monomoy separated from Morris Island: it was now accessible only by boat.

Protracted hearings were held in the 1960s on the issue of reclassifying Monomoy:

> *One Washington official told us last Friday that he honestly thought that more emotional concern had been expressed in some quarters of the government last week over the issue of Monomoy than over the terrible events in Viet Nam.*[241]

The old Monomoy Point Coast Guard Station, blown up by the navy, 1960s. Coast Guard coxswain Bernie Webber thought the place was haunted by the ghosts of long-gone surf men. *Photo courtesy of the Chatham, Massachusetts Historical Society.*

The debate raged for years. "Wilderness system status will help assure that this relatively tiny area will remain forever wild," the *New York Times* stated on January 12, 1967.

In 1969, the Audubon Society and private owners were offering beach buggy rides to Monomoy. Yet the following year, when 97 percent of Monomoy was declared a wilderness area, motorized vehicles were banned. Pets, bicycles, camping, hunting, shooting, fires and the picking of plants were all banned.

Early in 1964, the U.S. Navy blew up the Monomoy Point Station. By 1980, Harley wrote, "there is nothing left except the beauty and the serenity of perhaps the most beautiful single place I have ever been on this earth."

A decade later, on a beautiful summer day, Dana Eldridge took his father, Wib, on a one-way trip to Monomoy. His father had loved Monomoy and had been lucky enough to live at a time when he could spend a good part of his life there in his camps. On Monomoy, Eldridge spread Wib's ashes.

"Being there will give him peace for all time, something we all crave," Eldridge wrote.[242]

Monomoy has at last been given over to nature and to spirits.

THE GREAT BLACKOUT OF '65

During the early evening of November 9, 1965, Earle Hiscock was riding on the 5:15 p.m. Almeida Bus from Logan Airport to Cape Cod. He had just flown into Logan from New York. During Hiscock's journey of about an hour and a half, he watched as streetlights, and the lights in houses all along the route, dimmed and went dark. Could sunspots be responsible? he wondered. Moon flares? Did a student driver knock over a crucial pole?

Chatham lay illuminated only by a bright full moon when Hiscock got home to Puddle-By on Old Harbor Road.

"On Cape Cod, as everywhere else in the afflicted East, the bright Hunter's Moon shone down on a citizenry that took the abrupt phenomenon with good nature, curiosity and calm," the *Cape Codder* reported on November 11, 1965.

The lights came back on at 9:40 p.m.

The next day, contemplating future blackouts during winter storms, people rushed out to buy candles, kerosene lamps, flashlights, batteries, Coleman stoves and lanterns. Local hardware stores took advantage of the panic and advertised blackout specials.

STRONG ISLAND

Victor Horst, a man who had made a fortune in Arthur Miller franchise dancing studios, had bought fifty-five-acre Strong Island in about 1951 for $30,000. The beautiful island in Pleasant Bay had previously been used as a hunting preserve, and it remained undeveloped except for Horst's house, which was built in the late '30s.[243]

It was said that when President Kennedy could no longer stand the crowds in Hyannis Port, he considered summering, during 1964, on Strong Island.[244]

Horst's nearest neighbors on Strong Island Road were often amused to see him traveling to and from the island in his amphibious car. They were not so amused when, in 1963, Horst unveiled the first of several schemes to subdivide the island. "It and others that followed were resisted by Chatham residents who feared pollution of the surrounding waters and who wanted the island kept in its natural condition."[245]

Meeting resistance to his subdivision plan, Horst sued the planning board at the end of 1965. A key glitch in his scheme was the unresolved question

The town rebuffed repeated attempts by Victor Horst, who had bought fifty-five-acre Strong Island in about 1951, to develop it. Ultimately, Horst sold most of the island to the Chatham Conservation Foundation, protecting it. *Original watercolor courtesy of artist Kathrine Lovell.*

of where residents, guests, suppliers and official vehicles might park while they were on the island.

In his final scheme, Horst proposed fifty-two houses with swimming pools, tennis courts and "other amenities of wealth." The $6 million cluster development plan would have required a zoning change that was rejected by voters.

In December 1974, while retaining the use of his own house and several acres around it, Horst sold most of Strong Island to the Chatham Conservation Foundation for $700,000—another victory for the growing conservation movement.

ALL ROADS LEAD TO THE HOJO

Something was flapping from the weather vane atop the Howard Johnson's takeout restaurant at the rotary. After studying it for a while, the manager, Don St. Pierre, hired a man named Willy Razina to scale the roof and get the item. It was a size 19A brassiere.[246]

Don, a graduate of Harwich High School, was twenty-one years old in 1961 when he took over the management of the restaurant after a year as assistant manager. This takeout HoJo was built in 1958 and joined a string of Howard Johnson's franchises on the Cape. Famous for its "28 Flavors" of ice cream, "3D Burgers" with their special sauce and fried clams, the restaurant with the orange roof was at the height of its success in the 1960s. Events such as a freshman class car wash were held in the HoJo's parking lot. The cost was one dollar per car, with fifty cents extra for white walls.

"It was where everybody met after the band concert," Don recalls. "The place was absolutely jammed."

The front of the building was made of glass and faced the rotary at the intersection of Stage Harbor Road and Main Street. A line of stools was pushed up to a counter attached to the front window; most diners, though, sat outside at the eight or ten picnic tables. The HoJo did not serve liquor.

Don, who had a dog named HoJo that liked to chase cars, led a troop of Explorer Scouts at the Doc Keene Scout Hall in his free time. He and the scouts went everywhere—hunting on North Beach, the stock car races, shooting, skiing, even to the battleship *Massachusetts* in Fall River. It was fortunate that he got along with young people, because the HoJo had become *the* place for young people to hang out.

"We'd go there every night," says Fred Byrne, who was fifteen during the summer of '67. "Half the time we didn't buy anything." Rick Smith's regular order was French fries and a glass of water. "That's all we could afford," he recalls.

On nights when Fred did buy something, he'd line up at the takeout window, order and head to one of the picnic tables set under big elms that shrouded the area. "The fog would come in on summer nights and it would drift down on the tables," he says.

Out in the parking lot, a light pole was embedded in a concrete slab. The light had a short, and if you touched the concrete, you got a minor shock. About twenty young people would line up holding hands and the one closest to the concrete slab would touch it, sending a jolt down the group. Fred hated it but, in the manner of teenagers, was always willing to join the electric conga line.

The appeal of the HoJo, for this underage summer crowd, was that "you were right on top of it, everything that was going on," Fred says. If you were looking for a beach party, the HoJo acted as the clearing house. Fred remembers animosity that boiled down to class warfare between the summer kids and the local kids. "We'd get in fights occasionally."

"Year-round kids were townies," Smith agrees. "People had the stigma. Somehow my brothers and sister and I were able to cross the line without a problem." Smith made lifelong friends both among the summer crowd at the yacht club and among his local schoolmates.

One evening in July, a local boy spotted one of Chatham's summer patrolmen—"rent-a-cops," as they were known—and he had an idea. He went back by the HoJo's dumpster and lit up one of his Camel unfiltered cigarettes. He then stuck the fuse of a firecracker into the unlit end of the cigarette, returned the firecracker to its box and set the box on the asphalt next to the dumpster. He was back at his spot at the picnic table when the burning Camel set off the box of firecrackers. It also ignited the rent-a-cop.

"He drew his gun and ran around like there was a big crime," the man recalls.

"It was just fun shenanigans," Don says.

Twins Jerry and Jeff Frank were also denizens of the HoJo. "Me and my brother, we used to hang out there," Jeff recalls.[247]

Growing up, Jerry and Jeff always dressed alike. As they advanced through the Chatham schools, they were so similar in appearance that their teachers made them wear nametags, Jerry recalls. By the summer of '67, the twins were twenty-three years old and used to date identical twin girls. On dates, Jerry and Jeff dressed alike and so did the girls. The quartet always made a splash when they entered restaurants looking like a Doublemint gum commercial.

Love Story

Don happened to notice a young woman who was a regular at the HoJo. She was Hannah Sheehan, who had been working for Mrs. Seymour over on Water Street for a few years now. Don asked an older woman who was a friend of Hannah if Hannah was "available." The response was encouraging. Don then asked Hannah for a date, at a cookout on North Beach.

Dates on the beach were not what young Johannah Mary Sheehan from County Cork, Ireland, was used to. She was, in fact, used to more sophisticated fare like the New York theatre or movies.[248]

Hannah had come to Chatham with Gladys Seymour, the widow of the fifteenth president of Yale. Charles Seymour had died in August 1963 at his summer home in the Old Village; Hannah, who was about twenty, joined the Seymour family the following year and ran errands and helped out at Mrs. Seymour's many parties. During the school year, Mrs. Seymour remained in New Haven, where her son, Charles Jr., was a professor of art history at Yale, and during the summer Mrs. Seymour returned to her home on Water Street.

Water Street. The name says it all. Stand on the street and to the east you can see Chatham Harbor. Swivel your head and to the west you can see the Mill Pond. It is possible to swim at either end of Water Street, and the sunsets over the Mill Pond are spectacular.

Hannah, who had grown up on a dairy farm, had come to New Haven originally because her aunt was living there. It was fun to be in a city so near to Manhattan. But in Chatham, Hannah loved the beach and spent much of her free time there or, on Friday evenings, at band concerts. During her summers with the Seymours, she came to know the Yale crowd in the Old Village and also her neighbors on Water Street.

At the end of Water Street, on a bluff overlooking the Mill Pond, was the 1858 house the Porches. This house, set back behind a white picket fence and Dorothy Perkins roses, was once a dry goods store owned by Mary Gusta Young that Joseph Lincoln made famous in his novel *Mary Gusta*. Mrs. Young's daughter, Avis Chase, inherited the house, and when she died in 1953, Mrs. Chase left the house to the Philadelphia YWCA to allow young women of that city to enjoy one- or two-week vacations in Chatham. Although she stipulated that those vacationing be white, Protestant women, the trustees of the YWCA said it would be illegal to enforce that rule, and they allowed women of all races and religions to use the house, which was converted into many guest rooms.

In the 1960s, this landmark Greek revival building in the Old Village was a gift shop and inn called the Calico Cat. When it was built in 1840, it was Hallet's Store. *Photo by the author.*

At the other end of Water Street, facing the harbor, were the three buildings of Hawes House, now in its final decade of operation. Just around the corner was a gift shop called the Calico Cat, in a striking Greek revival building.

Halfway up the street was the 1730 house that Esther Johnson, the first wife of F. Seward Johnson, an heir to Johnson & Johnson, would buy at a tax sale in '67 and restore. The house stood out with its whimsical Queen Anne additions, including a turret. That house would later be bought by the Bingham family of Louisville newspaper fame. Also on the street, the architectural historian Clair Baisly ran a copper craft shop from her house, which was built later than most of the other houses, in 1935.

Hannah's date with Don on North Beach, with other young people, was a success. Someone built a fire, and they roasted hot dogs, hamburgers and sweet corn. On Valentine's Day, Don drove down to New Haven to propose to Hannah, and she accepted.

Don and Hannah were married in October 1967 at Chatham's Holy Redeemer Church, with Hannah's two brothers flying from Ireland for the wedding. Don and his younger brother, Norman, were known as "the two Saints." The following April, Don left the HoJo and went into business with Norman, who had bought Slim Hutchings's gas station in North Chatham.

"For the Times They Are a Changing"

The sounds of Chatham were changing again. Take the beach. With the rise of portable transistor radios, people could tuck radios into their beach bags and listen to music on the beach. As you trudged along, digging your bare feet through the burning sand to the cooler sand below, the music changed at every blanket.

In the ice cream shack at Ridgevale Beach, a teenager with a Beatles "mop top" haircut sweeps sand off the wooden floor while he's not scooping ice cream or selling Cokes. From another transistor, Tommy Roe sings his 1966 hit "Oh, Sweet Pea, Come On and Dance with Me," and a six-year-old girl who just ordered an ice cream cone mishears it as "oh, sweepy"—music to sweep by. The teenager scoops pistachio ice cream into a cone, pats it down and then gives it a quick lick before handing it to the child.

"It was dripping," he says as she gapes at him. Halfway up the road to their rental house on Cranberry Lane, the girl catches up with her father. He has been plodding along with rubber raft, beach chairs and

Barbara Aaronson hugs her brother-in-law, William J. Carey, on Ridgevale Beach while the author looks on in August 1966. The Rhode Island family was renting a cottage on Cranberry Lane within walking distance of the Nantucket Sound beach. *Photo courtesy of the author.*

towels. He stops. "He licked it," she says as she sticks out the ice cream cone, which, un-tasted, has melted all over her hand and wrist. Setting down the raft and the beach chairs, her father takes the cone. He eats it in one gulp.

WHAT'S ANOTHER BOMB?

Even though the air force no longer bombed Monomoy, it seemed that someone was always crazy about setting off incendiary devices near Cape Cod. This time, it was the oil industry, looking for oil off the coast. The result was a massive fish kill during 1966.

A year later, lobbyists for Cape Cod had howled loudly enough to stop the practice. Bills had been filed that would prevent mineral exploration and development off the coast. Yet "the specter of oil rigs on our horizon and oil spewing into our waters still persists," the 1967 *Report of the Town Officers* warns.

PUFF THE DRAGON

Mary Jane. Reefer. Grass. Weed. Something shifted in the national zeitgeist between 1966 and 1967. Look through any school's yearbooks: often the graduates of 1966 still have a groomed appearance. In 1967, however, they look like they stuck their fingers into electric light sockets. The four Beatles, on the cover of their psychedelic 1967 album, *Sergeant Pepper's Lonely Hearts Club Band*, are now sporting longer hair, mustaches and beards. The Summer of Love was on in Haight Ashbury in San Francisco, and its effects trickled east to Chatham, where, during July and August, "seemingly endless days of fog" interrupted the monotonous rain.[249]

"During 1967 the narcotic problem was brought to the forefront when arrests were made," Police Chief David Nickerson wrote in his annual report. Southeastern Massachusetts was "high on the list of marijuana users," he added in a sentence rife with unintended irony. The following year, he dubbed alcohol and narcotics "a real social problem."

For a whole generation, restrooms seemed to be a place to get up to no good, probably because they offered a person privacy under the guise of answering "calls of nature." Kids drank and smoked pot in the bathrooms of the HoJo.

A cartoon called *Brooks Looks* in the *Cape Codder* on November 2, 1967, shows a mother reading a letter from her daughter to her husband. "She wants us to send money for pot, 'the Pill'—and her teddy bear!" the astonished woman says.

School nurse Margaret Guild chaired a new committee on drug education in the schools. "In this country every community should be made aware of the dangers to our children and actively study the situation, institute a program and follow it through," the committee said in the 1967 *Report of the Town Officers*. During the 1967–68 school year, Guild's health education curriculum revolved around venereal disease and drug abuse.

Yet "Chatham would have been kind of slow to latch onto all that," Fred Byrne believes. "The attitude of anti-establishment never really hit so hard here as it did where I was raised" in Westchester County, New York.

Along with drug abuse came overdose. In the statistical reports of ambulance runs for the late '60s are several cases of drug reactions or overdoses. Rick Smith remembers two kids—one of them younger than he—dying of heroin overdoses.

THE WAR COMES HOME—AGAIN

The *Cape Codder* was now running a column called "Vietnam News." In it, a writer begs schoolmates of any of the "boys" who are now in Vietnam to write to them. In words that evoke Edna Matteson and her World War II *Home Fires* letters, the columnist writes, "While they are overseas this means more to them than anything else we could send them for Christmas."

OH, MAN, GET THAT THING OUTTA MY HAIR

Bugs. Bugs have, since time immemorial, flown, crawled, stung, bitten, sucked and dangled from webs.

Take wood ticks. "The problems of ticks should be made available to everyone—summer visitors and local citizens as well," wrote Harold C. Eldredge, the town's moth superintendent in the 1967 *Report of the Town Officers*. Eldredge made something of a study of ticks in 1967. Ticks had eight legs, like spiders. Their life span was 380 days. They could live for 320 days without eating and for 7 days under water. "So you can see he is tougher than the Viet Cong, and DDT is the best insecticide known until now to combat this insect." (DDT would be banned in 1972.)

In 1969, a new pest arrived: the "spotted tussock moth." This bit of natural nastiness hatched its eggs on the underside of oak leaves. Later, "they crawl on the sides of houses, and buildings, finding a place for the winter." By October 15, they were bedded down in cocoons.

One bit of good news: the wood tick was under study at the University of Massachusetts. "All the habits of the tick have to be known, especially where it winters," Eldredge concluded.

"CALL THE VATICAN, I DON'T CARE"

In the late '60s, Richard Costello and his friend George Payne were working the Boston restaurant scene. During high school, Payne had trained as a bartender and cook at the old New Yorker Restaurant on Main Street, a hangout for the servicemen during World War II. In 1968, Payne and Costello opened their own restaurant in that same spot, calling it the Chatham Squire.

"We just wanted to sell hot dogs and beers and have fun," Costello reminisces. "It took a while to understand we weren't just kids playing in the sandbox. It was business."[250]

When Payne and Costello arrived in Chatham, they "looked like hippies with beards and long hair and nobody liked us," Payne recalls. "Business was very slow until we wrote a sign on dirty old paper and hung it outside: lobster, steamers, corn-on-the-cob, 10-ounce glass of draft beer, $3.95."

The pivotal year of the 1960s was 1968. The year began with the January 31 Tet Offensive in Vietnam. On April 4, Martin Luther King Jr. was assassinated; on June 5, Robert F. Kennedy was assassinated. On November 5, Richard Milhous Nixon was elected president. The musical *Hair* began its run of 1,742 performances on Broadway.

"We were blessed when we first opened," Costello says. "We didn't have a lot. The first season seven or eight worked for room and board and tips. All we did was work. We got to play for four months with whatever we had left over."

Jerry and Jeff Frank, well known as the "Elvis Twins," were among the first to step through the door of the Squire on its first day.

"I can see it clear as a bell," Jerry recalls. "We went in the afternoon. They had a huge line of people. We got in front, said we had to use the bathroom."

The Squire quickly became the in-place for the of-age crowd. "It was a good time back then," one newcomer to Chatham, a commercial

"We looked like hippies with beards and long hair and nobody liked us," George Payne recalled about the year 1968, when he and Richard Costello arrived in Chatham to open the Chatham Squire. *Photo by the author.*

fisherman, says. "The Squire was the place to be. We mourned it in the winter when it was closed."

Back in the '60s and '70s, "a lot of people fetched up here. It was kind of our little oyster, our little playground," he recalls. The fishermen used to show up at 4:00 or 5:00 p.m. and drink until about 8:00 p.m. Although they played bridge, they made a rowdy crowd.

Certain events are legendary. Like the night somebody may have danced naked on the bar. Or the time people say an officer of the law was tossed—or fell—out through the front window.

Payne was present during what he dubs "the riot." He says it has been exaggerated—"It was just all college kids standing around." And he was tending bar the night "the fishermen decided to put all their boots on top of my piano and light them on fire," ending his dream of a piano bar.

For a while the Squire served breakfast after the bar shut down—from 1:00 to 3:00 a.m. Costello called it "the last chance saloon," with half the people sitting on the other half's laps.

Richard Costello (left) and George Payne, founders of the Chatham Squire, during the restaurant's fortieth anniversary in 2008. The pair is still running the well-known Main Street watering hole. *Photo by the author.*

The back bar is where 480 bras were eventually tossed onto the walls, as the story goes, by women baring their breasts for a free shot of tequila. "We used to take them off every year and wash them because they'd get dusty," Costello says of the bras. "One time they came out in a big ball."

The remaining bras, which Costello calls "art," offend some. One day, two nuns walked out after studying the painting over the raw bar showing a bearded sailor cupping the nude breast of a girl with long blonde hair. "Call the Vatican, I don't care!" Costello says about the incident.

THE END OF THE '60S

During the last week in May 1969, a pair of former drug addicts named Phil and Bill described for two hundred parents and concerned citizens at the Chatham Memorial Auditorium how they had fallen down the dark ladder from drink to marijuana to heroin. At the bottom rung was a jail cell. One person asked how a parent could possibly influence her son to stay away from drugs when she couldn't even lure him into cutting his hair?

"The speakers admitted that at Chatham High School they had had difficulty in determining who was a girl and who was a boy in some cases," the paper reported.[251]

Hair was one of the great generational divides of the 1960s. Rick Smith remembers the high school principal "going through hell" over the hair issue. "He would expel kids if they didn't get a haircut," Smith recalls. Yet parents eventually saw the long hair as a freedom of expression issue. It was no accident that the hit 1968 Broadway musical was named *Hair*.

Just before the summer of 1969 began, one of Chatham's residents died in a manner that remains unsolved. Monday, June 2, was a cloudy day, with thunderstorms likely in the evening. News accounts differ as to the details, but either fifty-eight-year-old Elizabeth Warner's husband or the Chatham police found her dead in her home overlooking Pleasant Bay in Chatham Port at about 5:00 p.m.

Chatham police sergeant Roderick MacDonald took charge of the investigation. Eventually, Mrs. Warner's death certificate would list the cause of death as "asphyxia due to strangulation—by ligature." Unlike the death, a decade earlier, of fifty-nine-year-old Walter Munford, the head of U.S. Steel, whose stabbing was ruled a self-inflicted accident, Mrs. Warner's death remains a mystery.

A MOON WALK AND VIETNAM

In early July 1969, the Pollock Rip lightship, which had been anchored for decades seven miles southeast of Chatham Light, simply sailed away. No longer would Chatham residents, when the wind was tilted in a certain direction, "hear that mournful blast…a deep-throated 3.5 second blast every 36 seconds that was a great comfort to commercial fishermen and many other ships passing off shore."[252] No longer would a forty-four-foot lifeboat shove off from the Chatham Fish Pier on Thursdays to bring the men on the lightship mail and provisions.

The lightship was replaced by a lighted buoy.

The light in the Chatham Light, too, was replaced with a brilliant, 2,465,000-candlepower beam with a geographic range of fifteen miles and a luminous range of twenty-five miles. The cast-off lens was given to the Chatham Historical Society, where it remains on display.

On July 10, Cape Cod Hospital kicked off a $6 million fund drive. Senator Edward M. Kennedy was one of the honorary co-chairs, along with Governor Francis Sargent. But ten days later, Kennedy had more pressing issues—the publicity that resulted when he drove off what would become a famous little bridge on Chappaquiddick, drowning Mary Jo Kopechne.

On the evening of July 20, Chatham's photographer, Dick Kelsey, stationed himself in front of his television set with his camera at the ready. That evening, shortly after 10:30 p.m., when *Apollo 11* astronaut Neil Armstrong stepped onto the moon, Kelsey began shooting. Two of his photos—of Armstrong and Buzz Aldrin planting a flag on the moon and of President Richard Nixon talking on the telephone to the moon walkers—were published in the *Lower Cape Cod Chronicle* the following Thursday.

An editorial in the paper noted that while man's spirit was "ennobled" by the flight, it asked: what next? Travel agent bookings for moon flights?

A few days later, Chatham got a taste of the senseless war in Vietnam when it learned that army specialist fourth class Arthur Allison of Cedar Street had died on July 16 in a helicopter accident in Vietnam. The 1966 graduate of Chatham High was twenty years old and had served in the army since April 1968, with the last five months in Vietnam.[253]

"The guy could swim under water forever," Rick Smith remembers about the older boy. "He would bring up a quahog. His hand would be black with mud."

The Reverend Carlyle Smith officiated at a military service at the First Congregational Church.

Ultimately, in addition to Allison, two other of Chatham's boys would die in Vietnam. John Aulde Sickel III was shot, and Thomas C. Nickerson was killed in combat in March 1967.[254]

GOIN' DOWN TO YASGUR'S FARM

At 6:00 a.m. on Friday, August 15, Rick Smith, who was then sixteen, met three of his friends in the parking lot of the HoJo. Rick's older sister, Heather, had already headed to Bethel, New York, with her own friends. Rick's family didn't know that he was also planning to go to Max Yasgur's six-hundred-acre farm, but he didn't think that would be a problem.[255]

Rick, who was between his sophomore and junior years at Chatham High, was playing keyboard in a band, Times of Creation, which had performed at the class of '68 prom. Three years earlier, he and his friends Jack and Tom Moye had formed a trio called the Hillwilliams—named as homage to the popular TV show *The Beverly Hillbillies*. Jack played the banjo, Tom played guitar and Rick was on drums. Following that, Rick played percussion in the school band, marching at the Fourth of July parade in 1968. His group also performed for Saturday night dances sponsored by the church at the community center. On at least one occasion, Fred Byrne had substituted on the guitar for a missing band member.

Rick's summer jobs included washing dishes and, one summer, working for Joe Buckley. They called themselves Buckley's Butchers, and their job was mowing graveyards. After a day of hand-trimming the grass around all the gravestones, Rick's hand would be sore. But this morning in August, Smith was concentrating on stowing his gear in the VW bus. He had tucked into his knapsack a couple of bags of chips, a canteen of water, a pocketknife with a can opener attachment and three cans of SpaghettiOs.

"I figured I'd eat them out of the can," Rick says.

The group set off with Bobby Olsen at the wheel to begin the drive of over 350 miles. After several hours, they hit the 20-mile traffic jam on Route 17B. Eventually, Rick, his friends and about a half million other young people reached Max Yasgur's farm, the site of the Woodstock Festival, "An Aquarian Exposition: 3 Days of Peace & Music."

"There was a great group of Chatham people there," he recalls. "We all sort of met." Ray Kane had a huge army tent that became their gathering point. Amazingly, Rick ran into his sister Heather in the crowd.

The festival is now legendary for its mud, lack of sanitary facilities and lack of food. But those who were there say the music and the fact that they were at *the* pivotal event of a generation made up for that. Rick loved hearing The Who and Mountain's Leslie West. Both Rick and Heather were among the diehards who heard Jimi Hendrix play "Fire," "Purple Haze," "Hey Joe" and "The Star-Spangled Banner" during his long set early on Monday morning.

Back in Chatham, Rick had to face a different kind of music when his family learned where he had been.

And yes, he did eat those SpaghettiOs. "I shared them," he says. "It was Woodstock."

HELL, NO, WE WON'T GO

No doubt it was dirty in those small houses. Bowls with smears of ketchup would have sat on the kitchen counters; a pan with crusts of beans or brown rice sat on the stove.

The windows would have been open against the heat of August; perhaps the inhabitants of the houses slept on mattresses tossed directly on the floors. A haze of smoke would hover in the air, and ashtrays overflowed with stubs of joints. A dusty HiFi would have held a stack of Grateful Dead albums.

It was into this counterculture haze that police officers from Chatham, Orleans and Brewster ventured in late August. The coordinated pot busts took place in Orleans and Brewster, netting twenty-one longhaired young people wearing dirty jeans and love beads. Three dealers were in the mix, police reported.

The *Cape Codder* was running a serial on "lost" kids—the first in the wave of the baby boomers who now, at twenty, were drifting and had a long history of drug abuse. Yet at a meeting of the nonresident taxpayers in late August, Police Chief David Nickerson spoke about the town's modest drug problem.[256] Of greater concern at that meeting was the presence of heaped-up seaweed on two town beaches. Selectman Robert McNeece said the seaweed was not being removed "because it helped hold the beach together during winter storms."

That month, Abigail McCarthy, the estranged wife of Minnesota senator Eugene McCarthy—a presidential candidate in 1968—bought an early nineteenth-century full Cape on Stage Harbor Road. Abigail began renovating the house to make it a summer home for her four college-age children.

THE MAGIC STILL LINGERS

In retrospect, some people place the cultural end of the '60s in August 1974, when Richard Nixon resigned from the presidency. Yet to contemporary observers, it seemed that, indeed, the '60s were ending on December 31, 1969.

"The decade that now departs will be well remembered, to be sure, but it would require a lush sentimentalism indeed to squeeze out an honest tear of nostalgia for its passing," William S. White wrote in the *Cape Cod Standard-Times* on December 31, 1969. He goes on to condemn rebels, dissenters, drugs, protestors, demonstrations, assassinations and unrest of all types.

Although the great blackout of '65 had initially been blamed on UFOs, an editorial writer noted that the air force had recently announced that it was dropping its search for flying saucers. For some inexplicable reason, people at the end of the '60s were no longer prone to seeing UFOs.

Although "the old Cape Cod of shipwrecks and whales seems a bit distant now…the shadows of the past still fall across the narrow land to remind us that things may not have changed so much after all."[257]

Cape Cod was still a magical place, attesting perhaps more to the legerdemain of the guidebook writers than to reality. It was a place where the air is "clear and clean," where ponds and streams remain "relatively unpolluted," the streets are "free of litter" and the town dump—"well, where else can you see a million seagulls at a time?"[258] A guidebook writer still propagated that old canard: "They say it snows very little on the Cape and they are right."

In 1968, the Chatham selectmen boasted about a summer article in the *Cape Cod Standard-Times* that said, in part, "If a tourist were restricted to visiting one Cape Cod town which may best fill his mental image of this famed vacation area, it would be Chatham."

By 1969, the Chatham fishing fleet consisted of thirty-five long-line vessels that brought in 4.2 million pounds of fish with a value of $706,000. The observation deck above the unloading area was "a visitor's special treat at Chatham: the pier features an observation deck…that gives the tourist and photographer a ringside seat." In fact, the pier had become an attraction that rivaled the Chatham Light. "You'll see many of the town's street signs have an extra directional marker to help you find it."[259]

Commercialism, the article continued, in the form of superhighways, neon signs, pizza shops, blaring music and clam shacks, had bypassed Chatham.

And where was the hot dog on this list? No one cared about hot dog stands anymore. After all, the town had strengthened its original 1957 zoning law

"Why not beautify the spot and point out to tourists something of its history?" asked town booster Heman Harding in 1916. In the decades that followed, the optical machines brought in enough change to maintain the area by the town's most popular attraction, Chatham Light. *Photo by the author.*

in 1969, a time when "the poisoning of our air and waters" and the "brutal bulldozing of our land—for what is all-too-often termed progress" were decried. The first Earth Day would be celebrated in April 1970.

By the end of the '60s, Heman Harding's 1912 vision of Chatham Light as a tourist attraction still held strong. "If any particular acre of Chatham soil were chosen to represent the seafaring trade of the peninsula, I'd vote for Chatham Light," one guidebook writer proclaimed. "Beautiful and moody in any season, the view from the bluff is a fine way to feel the pulse of Cape Cod."

Notes

Introduction

1. By 1963, with the building of Our Lady of Grace, Chatham would have seven churches and a Christian Science Reading Room.
2. Monbleau, *Home Song*, 98. Mutt's niece, Barbara Townson Weller, remembers her uncle and Thornton Wilder.
3. Ibid.

Wartime at Home

4. Interviews with Robert S. "Bob" Hardy Sr., October 2006 and February 2010.
5. Commemorative folder containing letters, news clips and photographs of Robert Scott Brown's career, Chatham Historical Society.
6. Monbleau, *Home Song*, 70.
7. Lincoln, *Bradshaws of Harniss*, 197–98. Although Lincoln made up the names of his fictional towns, it is possible to read the books imagining them set in any Cape Cod town.
8. *Chatham Main Street School*, 15.
9. *Cape Cod Standard-Times*, December 9, 1941.
10. *Chatham Monitor*, December 11, 1941.
11. Monbleau, *Home Song*, 70.
12. Baisly, *Cape Cod Architecture*, 51.
13. *Cape Cod Standard-Times*, May 24, 1940.
14. Interview with Reginald L. "Reggie" Nickerson, October 2009.
15. Maddeningly, the *Monitors* for the entire year of 1940 are missing. It would have been poignant to read Alice Guild's account of her friend's accident.
16. Minnie Buck was given the job of puttying the windows as "a filling job it was asserted should come easily to her." Unpublished paper on the Old Atwood House, Chatham Historical Society.

17. *New York Times*, June 4, 1939.
18. Monbleau, *Home Song*, 74. June James MacDonald said her Native American family was "met with every kind of discrimination you could think of." MacDonald's brother, Staff Sergeant Roland Wallace James, was killed in France in 1944.
19. Urofsky, *Brandeis*, 737.
20. "'The People's Attorney': Family Life," Brandeis University Library, lts.brandeis.edu/research/archives-speccoll/exhibits/brandeis/family/family.html.
21. Urofsky, *Brandeis*, 660.
22. *New York Times*, June 4, 1939.
23. Urofsky, *Brandeis*, 733.
24. *Chatham Monitor*, July 27, 1939.
25. At some point in 1939, Doc Keene delivered a baby named Millie. "Where in hell is that baby's head?" he was supposed to have uttered during delivery, according to a note scribbled on an undated news clip at the Chatham Historical Society.
26. Lincoln, *Bradshaws of Harniss*, 84.
27. *New York Times*, June 15, 1941.
28. *Chatham Monitor*, January 2, 1941.
29. Ibid., January 9, 1941.
30. *Cape Cod Standard-Times*, March 28, 1939.
31. Ibid., April 29, 1940.
32. *New York Times*, June 15, 1941.
33. Long after Harold Dunbar's death in 1953, this gag, more than his long painting career, seems to be what he is remembered for.
34. Cape Codders "are more cosmopolitan than city folk could know," Eleanor Early wrote in 1936. Yet the joke about Cape Cod being inhabited by idiots persists. In the 1984 film *Splash*, Tom Hanks is dropped off by a New York cab on a Cape Cod beach. A mad scientist introduces his local helpers to Hanks as "the moron twins." "We're not twins," one of them retorts.
35. All information on the Reynolds case comes from the *Cape Cod Standard-Times* of July 31, 1941. While the case made front-page headlines in that newspaper, the *Chatham Monitor* remained mum.
36. *Chatham Monitor*, July 24, 1941.
37. *Report of the Town Officers*, 1941.
38. *New York Times*, August 11, 1941.
39. *Oracle*, March 22, 1973.
40. Lincoln, *Bradshaws of Harniss*, 193.
41. Interview with Joseph A. "Joe" Nickerson, December 2006. He and Louise eventually married—about a year after they had planned.
42. Monbleau, *Home Song*, 34.
43. *Chatham Monitor*, December 11, 1941.
44. Burling, *Birth of the Cape*, 4.
45. Lincoln, *Bradshaws of Harniss*, 217.
46. The fact that the lights remained on in Atlantic City in 1942 gave the enemy a tremendous advantage in that it could see tankers and freighters silhouetted against the city.

47. D'Entremont, *Lighthouses of Massachusetts*, 174.

48. *Prime Time Cape Cod*, August 1995.

49. *Chatham Monitor*, December 18, 1941.

50. *Cape Cod Standard-Times*, December 22, 1941.

51. Much of this information comes from a scrapbook kept by Margaret Guild, now in the private collection of her nephew Gene Guild, and from interviews with Gene Guild in December 2009 and February 2010.

52. Margaret Guild, who became, in later years, a major force in Chatham's schools and in the Visiting Nurses Association, would care for her mother, Alice, at home until she died at the age of ninety-nine in 1975. Margaret would die in 1979.

53. In the early 1950s, the Picketts would return to Chatham and build a house one hundred feet from where the guard shack once stood. Growing up, Lonnie Pickett Jr. remembers evidence of tight security there during the war. "We used to play in the machine gun emplacements," he says. "The buildings were gone. There were fox holes and sandbags." From interviews with Pickett, June 2007 and November 2009.

54. *Boston Herald*, July 23, 1941.

55. *Cape Cod Standard-Times*, May 14, 1942.

56. Nathan, *Journal for Josephine*, 72–73.

57. D'Entremont, *Lighthouses of Massachusetts*, 181.

58. Nathan, *Journal for Josephine*, 82.

59. Ibid., 25.

60. Monbleau, *Home Song*, 64.

61. Stuart Stearns, who was born in Hyannis but was working in Rahway, New Jersey, recalls on two occasions in 1942 driving after dark to Point Pleasant on the Jersey Shore. On the horizon, he could see "a glow, a ball of light" caused by a burning tanker that a German U-boat had torpedoed.

62. Elinor Miller, *Prime Time Cape Cod*, August 1995.

63. *Report of the Town Officers*, 1942.

64. All quotes from Matteson are from her *Home Fires* Chatham newsletter in the Chatham Historical Society.

65. *Report of the Town Officers*, 1942.

66. Anita Freeman later became Anita Eldridge.

67. *Cape Cod Chronicle*, September 25, 2002.

68. D'Entremont, *Lighthouses of Massachusetts*, 174.

69. *Cape Cod Chronicle*, September 25, 2002.

70. LORAN is affected by meteorological effects and changes in the reflecting ionosphere. Now considered outdated, it has been replaced by the Global Positional System (GPS), which is immune to these effects.

71. *Cape Cod Voice*, August 26–September 24, 2004.

72. *Prime Time Cape Cod*, August 1995.

73. Stallknecht, "Something of My Past." The minister who had approved the installation of the first mural in 1933 was the young Reverend Franklin Pierce Cole, Stallknecht's friend and booster.

74. *Time*, September 9, 1957.

75. Interestingly, Hardy's mother, Josephine, who had inherited a two-hundred-acre farm in West Chatham, sold the land that is now Chatham Airport together with all of the lots on White Pond for $2,000 to Wilfred Berube, who developed the airport.
76. *New York Times*, May 9, 1943.
77. Interview with Harry Cutts, January 2010.
78. *Cape Cod Standard-Times*, October 9, 1943.
79. Much of this information comes from a telephone interview with Schalizki in November 2009 and in-person interviews in May 2008, when Schalizki returned to Chatham for the first time in nearly sixty-five years. Accompanied by his former boss, Dick Lumpkin, he revisited his workstation in what is now the Chatham Marconi Maritime Center (CMMC). "We worked hard, we played hard, and I guess we could say we enjoyed the war," Schalizki said. "It's a funny thing to say, but we knew the aims, we knew what we had to do to end the conflict."
80. Rose Acres Inn "was known far and wide for its Sunday night lobster buffets." Elinor Miller, *Prime Time Cape Cod*, August 1995.
81. General background information on the German U-boats and communications comes from many sources listed in the bibliography.
82. Unpublished paper by Lois Wardner Wonders, who served in the WAVES in 1945. In CMMC collection.
83. Budiansky, *Battle of Wits*, 357. Chatham Station C was apparently the sole interceptor and transmitter of German U-boat intelligence.
84. Specific information on Chatham Station C was gleaned through interviews with Schalizki, Lumpkin and Richard Kraycir, CMMC board member.
85. The Town of Chatham's purchase and stewardship of the historic Marconi station complex attests to its interest and affection for the unit. Recently, the nonprofit CMMC has been restoring the property and has leased the operations building, the scene of wartime activities. The group plans to open the building as a museum for the 2010 season.
86. While Dick Lumpkin, who died in 2008, had received, through the Freedom of Information Act, some archival information about the navy's role at the radio station, much more material is yet to be released and investigated, according to Richard Kraycir of the CMMC.
87. Throughout the novel, seventy-year-old Zenas Bradshaw suffers from a cardiac problem that causes extreme attacks of vertigo and collapse followed by periods of doctor-ordered bed rest. One wonders if Lincoln, who died of a heart attack shortly after the book was published, modeled Bradshaw's symptoms on his own.
88. The Chatham Honor Roll contains the names of about three hundred men and women.
89. Both Edna May and her sister, Grace Hardy, went deaf in their twenties. Their nephew Bob Hardy speculates that typhoid might have been the culprit. While Edna worked in the library, Grace taught lip reading to deaf students in Boston. The women shared a house on Main Street that overlooked the little Mill Pond.
90. Ives, *Beacon for Chatham*, 48.
91. *Chatham News*, May 8, 1968.

92. *New Bedford Standard-Times*, September 14, 1944.

93. Snow, *Pilgrim Returns*, 370.

94. Interview with Reggie Nickerson, October 2008.

95. About 1977 the freight station was restored and moved from Stallknecht's yard to the Chatham Historical Society. Today, visitors can enter the "Mural Barn" directly from the Atwood House Museum.

96. Snow, *Pilgrim Returns*, 370.

97. *Report of the Town Officers*, 1945.

98. *New York Times*, March 4, 1945.

99. Summer resident Elinor Miller recalled that the sound of bombing was "a permanent background to the summer frolics of vacationers." *Prime Time*, August 1995.

100. McElheny, *Insisting on the Impossible*, 137–38.

101. After the war, Lumpkin's and Schalizki's paths diverged. Lumpkin went into the insurance business in Chatham. Schalizki, who met his future companion, Bob Davis, in the Biltmore Hotel in Providence in 1942, returned to Maryland, where he eventually settled into the real estate business.

102. *Prime Time*, August 1995.

103. "Someday mankind will be civilized enough to recognize that a woman is entitled to an identity completely her own and will allow her to retain her name, and not make her feel that she is merely a part of her husband's property," Virginia wrote to her lawyer on September 20, 1945. From an unpublished paper in the Chatham Historical Society.

104. The Christian Science church, today's Unitarian Universalist, would not be built until 1958.

105. *Cape Cod Standard-Times*, August 20, 1945.

106. Ibid.

107. Monbleau, *Home Song*, 28, 30.

108. Taylor, *Punch with Care*, 4. Between 1931 and 1951, Taylor published twenty-four entertaining Cape Cod mysteries that deftly explore the clashes in viewpoints between Cape Cod locals and their visitors.

109. Virginia Harding McGrath practiced what she preached. To the Chatham Historical Society, she donated twenty-three boxes of her father's legal files, ten boxes of her own records and thirty-six boxes—198 linear feet—of materials from her second husband Thomas McGrath's printing company. The collection forms an invaluable record of Chatham.

110. *Chatham Main Street School*, 13.

111. Webber, *Lifeboatmen*, 38.

112. Snow, *Pilgrim Returns*, 345.

113. Ibid., 358.

114. Ibid., 371.

115. *New Bedford Standard-Times*, November 10, 1946.

116. Eldridge, *Once Upon Cape Cod*, 50.

117. *New York Times*, June 8, 1947.

118. O'Connell, *Becoming Cape Cod*, 104.

119. It would take the intervention, in 1968, of Esther Johnson, wife of J. Seward Johnson, an heir to the Johnson & Johnson fortune, to get the Louchheims into the club. Louchheim, *My Crowd*, 87.

120. *Cape Codder*, September 4, 1969, interview with Katie Louchheim.

121. Faderman, *Believe in Women*, 246. Reynard became Gildersleeve's companion in the mid-1940s after the 1942 death of Gildersleeve's previous companion, Caroline Spurgeon. Gildersleeve nicknamed Reynard "Skipper," supposedly because Reynard so resembled her seafaring grandfather.

122. In 1934, Reynard published *The Narrow Land: Folk Chronicles of Old Cape Cod*. A paperback edition of the book was published by the Chatham Historical Society in 1968 and remains in print today.

123. Reynard, *Narrow Land*, 413.

124. A partial transcript of the hearing is in the Chatham Historical Society.

125. Harry Cutts remembers that his family used to watch the dive bombers strafe Monomoy from the front porch of their Champlain Road home. "The bombs sounded like thumps and you could see some smoke and sand from the bombs," Cutts said. As the planes swooped, they heard machine guns, too. February 2010 interview.

126. Gildersleeve, *Many a Good Crusade*, 415.

OLD CAPE COD

127. Interview with Jan Woolf Bilhuber, January 2010.

128. Early, *Cape Cod Summer*, 260.

129. Interview with Nancy Husted Koerner, January 2010.

130. Every summer, the Hawes House hired seven waitresses; each girl had one day off a week.

131. Robert Aikman, "Cocktails at the Hawes House," www.haweshouse.org.

132. Tifft and Jones, *Patriarch*, 229.

133. Lincoln, *Cape Cod Yesterdays*, 46.

134. *Cape Codder*, January 17, 1954.

135. Eloise H. Smith, "History of Harbor Coves," 1990 pamphlet at the Chatham Historical Society.

136. O'Connell, *Becoming Cape Cod*, ix.

137. Jakle, Sculle and Rogers, *Motel in America*, 80. "Veterans had their own boon: whereas prewar mortgages had demanded 50 percent down payments and repayment in ten years, full mortgages repayable over thirty years enabled 3.75 million veterans to buy homes."

138. *Cape Codder*, September 31, 1951.

139. Eastward, Ho! job slips from the papers of printer Thomas McGrath at the Chatham Historical Society.

140. "TheCooksandTheLearnards as one word," 2003 pamphlet at the Chatham Historical Society.

141. *Cape Codder*, February 23, 1950.

142. Ibid., February 7, 1952.

143. Morgan, *Cape Cod Cottage*, 9.
144. Ibid.
145. Ibid., 23.
146. Ibid., 19.
147. *Cape Codder*, February 18, 1954.
148. *Cape Cod Beacon*, November 1937.
149. Swift, *Roosevelts and Royals*, 3.
150. Ibid. Tellingly, in her book *Passion and Prejudice: A Family Memoir*, Sallie Bingham of the wealthy newspaper family says that every summer her family rented a house in Chatham and became "just another big, middle-class family at the beach." What evidence does she cite for this? "We ate hot dogs at Howard Johnson and gorged on saltwater taffy." Bingham, *Passion and Prejudice*, 278.
151. *Cape Cod Beacon*, March 1938, 24.
152. *Cape Codder*, February 18, 1954.
153. O'Connell, *Becoming Cape Cod*, 97.
154. Finch, *Place Apart*, 374.
155. O'Connell, *Becoming Cape Cod*, 97.
156. Burling, *Birth of the Cape*, 4.
157. *Cape Codder*, January 21, 1954.
158. O'Connell, *Becoming Cape Cod*, 97.
159. *Cape Codder*, February 28, 1952.
160. Ibid., February 21, 1952.
161. Webber, *Lifeboatmen*, 43. Unless otherwise specified, information on the *Pendleton* comes from this source.
162. *CG 36500* was restored in 1981 and is listed on the National Register of Historic Places. It is now owned by the Orleans Historical Society, which docks it in Rock Harbor during the summer.
163. Eldridge, *Cape Cod Lucky*, 95.
164. *Cape Codder*, September 27, 1956.
165. Ibid., May 8, 1952.
166. Richardson's 1929 *The Gardener's Bed-Book*, 365 short essays, is considered a gardening classic and remains in print.
167. First Congregational Church brochure for the August 3, 1953 annual house tour.
168. *Cape Codder*, May 8, 1952.
169. Smith, *Patenting the Sun*, 25.
170. Interview with Gene Guild, February 2010.
171. Smith, *Patenting the Sun*, 37.
172. *Report of the Town Officers*, 1917.
173. Smith, *Patenting the Sun*, 158.
174. *Cape Codder*, September 4, 1952.
175. Ibid., August 9, 1956.
176. Ibid., May 21, 1959.
177. Kukil, *Plath Journals*, 129.
178. Ibid., 119.

179. Ibid., 139.

180. Hughes, *Birthday Letters*, 65–66.

181. FBI director J. Edgar Hoover estimated the number of Communists as one in every 1,814 citizens. Oshinsky, *Polio*, 146.

182. *Cape Codder*, September 13, 1951.

183. Delaney and Ward, "Radar Development," 147.

184. Interviews with Lonnie Pickett, June 2007 and November 2009.

185. In 2007, Roger Porter Denk, a Chatham summer resident since 1969, published a thriller called *Stepping Stones*, which heightens the mystery surrounding the radar site.

186. Delaney and Ward, "Radar Development," 167.

187. Lincoln Laboratory, a part of MIT, was instrumental in developing the SAGE system. The radar facilities were tied into the enormous Whirlwind computer in Cambridge through computer and telephone links. The SAGE stations therefore served as an early warning radar network that could dispatch interceptor jets to deal with intruders. The entire system was set up to study and prove a daring new concept that coupled radar sensing units with computers for analysis and control using digitized information sent over civilian telephone lines.

188. *Chatham Shopper News*, April 15, 1966.

189. *Cape Codder*, March 20, 1952.

190. 250th Anniversary Celebration Program, Eldredge Public Library.

191. *Chatham Shopper News*, April 15, 1966.

192. Ibid., September 24, 1953; Dunbar's death certificate.

193. *Cape Cod Chronicle*, October 10, 1985.

194. *Cape Codder*, February 10, 1955.

195. Ibid., August 31, 1954.

196. *Cape Cod Standard-Times*, April 1, 1951.

197. *Cape Codder*, August 26, 1954.

198. Ibid., September 2, 1954.

199. O'Connell, *Becoming Cape Cod*, 98.

200. *Cape Codder*, August 9, 1956.

201. Ibid., September 6, 1956.

202. Beatrice F.B. Desellar, "The Old House on Old Wharf Road," unpublished paper, June 6, 1979, located at the Chatham Historical Society.

203. In 1969, the play was filmed in France as *Trois Hommes sur un Cheval*. The play itself was revived in local theatres from time to time. In 1977, a local reviewer called it "sometimes simplistic, almost sophomoric." *Cape Cod Chronicle*, August 4, 1977.

204. Unpublished letter by John Cecil Holm, Chatham Historical Society.

205. Hunt, *Cape Cod Cookbook*, 84.

206. *Cape Cod Chronicle*, September 30, 1992.

207. Shirley Booth died in her North Chatham cottage in 1992 at the age of ninety-four. She was perhaps best known in recent decades as Hazel, the maid in a 1960s television show of that name.

208. Achilles, who served in the United States Foreign Service for over thirty years, was ambassador to Peru from 1956 to 1960. *New York Times*, April 15, 1986.

209. Lincoln, *Cape Cod Yesterdays*, 219.

210. Burrows, *Windmills*, 83.

211. Plans are underway for the mill to be up and running again in time for Chatham's 2012 tercentennial.

212. Alice Guild, *The Old Windmill* brochure.

213. Yacobian, *Cannon on Bassing Harbor*. All information about Cannon Hill comes from this illustrated monograph.

214. *Cape Cod Chronicle*, July 3, 1975.

215. *Cape Codder*, August 9, 1956.

216. Eldridge, *Cape Cod Lucky*, 27–28.

217. O'Connell, *Becoming Cape Cod*, 119.

218. Burling, *Birth of the Cape*, 14.

219. Ibid., 26.

220. *Cape Codder*, October 1, 1959.

221. Unless otherwise noted, information on Munford comes from the *New York Times*, September 24–29, 1959.

222. *Cape Codder*, October 1, 1959.

223. The S.S. Pierce affiliation lasted through 2008, when the Epicure, then a liquor store that sold S.S. Pierce brand liquors as well as others, changed hands.

The Age of Aquarius

224. Interview with Fred Byrne, February 2010.

225. *Chatham's Old Houses*, Book II, *Some More Old Chatham Houses*, 12–13.

226. O'Connell, *Becoming Cape Cod*, 105.

227. Ibid., 99.

228. Marjorie C. Griffin, "An Outline History of the First Congregational Church, Chatham, Massachusetts, 1664–1988," pamphlet, 32.

229. "The Sacred Service of Ordination," album in the private collection of Rick Smith.

230. Jonas, *History of Harding Shores*, 42.

231. Interview with John H. and Elizabeth M. Moye, January 2010.

232. Baisly, *Cape Cod Architecture*, 102.

233. *Cape Codder*, November 21, 1963.

234. Ibid., November 28, 1963.

235. To alter or tear down a house over seventy-five years old in Chatham, you must gain approval of the Chatham Historical Commission. In 2010, the commission estimates that well over one thousand houses fit into this category.

236. Finch, *Place Apart*, 368.

237. Reynard, *Narrow Land*, 253.

238. U.S. Fish & Wildlife Service, www.fws.gov.

239. Hartley was an editor for the *Cape Cod Times* and a childhood friend of the author Dana Eldridge.

240. Webber, *Lifeboatmen*, 25.

241. *Boston Globe*, 1963.

242. Eldridge, *Once Upon Cape Cod*, 112.

243. *Cape Cod Beacon*, April 1937.

244. O'Connell, *Becoming Cape Cod*, 109.

245. *New York Times*, December 26, 1974.

246. Interview with Donald St. Pierre, February 2010.

247. Interviews with Jeff and Jerry Frank, April 2008 and February 2010.

248. Interview with Hannah Sheehan St. Pierre, January 2010.

249. "They say that Chatham housewives regularly scoop off chunks of a good 'pea souper,' add leftovers and heat it up for lunch." Wood, *Cape Cod*, 265.

250. Interviews with Richard Costello and George Payne, June 2008.

251. *Lower Cape Cod Chronicle*, May 29, 1969.

252. *Cape Cod Standard-Times*, July 2, 1969.

253. *Lower Cape Cod Chronicle*, July 31, 1969.

254. Carlisle, *Weathering*, 150.

255. Interview with Rick Smith, December 2009.

256. *Cape Codder*, August 21, 1969.

257. Wood, *Cape Cod*, 21.

258. Ibid.

259. Ibid., 277–78.

Bibliography

BOOKS AND BROCHURES ON
CHATHAM AND CAPE COD

Baisly, Clair. *Cape Cod Architecture*. Orleans, MA: Parnassus Imprints, Inc., 1989.

Burling, Francis I. *The Birth of the Cape Cod National Seashore*. Plymouth, MA: Leyden Press, 1978.

Burrows, Fredrika A. *Windmills on Cape Cod and the Islands*. Taunton, MA: William S. Sullwold Publishing, Inc., 1978.

Cairn, North T. *By Monomoy Light: Nature and Healing in an Island Sanctuary*. Boston: Northeastern University Press, 2000.

Carlisle, Robert D.B. *Weathering a Century of Change: Chatham, Cape Cod: The Story of a Seaside Village 1900–2000*. Chatham, MA: Chatham Historical Society, 2000.

Chatham Main Street School: A Book of Memories. Chatham, MA: Chatham Elementary School Advisory Council, 1998.

Chatham's Old Houses. Books I to VI. Chatham, MA: Chatham Historical Society, 1962–67.

Coleman, Roslyn Bayha. *Sterling Old Stock*. N.p., 2009.

Corbett, Scott. *Cape Cod's Way: An Informal History*. New York: Thomas Y. Crowell Co., 1955.

———. *We Chose Cape Cod*. Orleans, MA: Parnassus Imprints, 1984.

Denk, Roger Porter. *Stepping Stones: A Novel*. Charleston, SC: Advantage, 2007.

Early, Eleanor. *And This Is Cape Cod!* Boston: Houghton Mifflin Co., 1936.

———. *Cape Cod Summer*. Boston: Houghton Mifflin Co., 1949.

Eldridge, Dana. *Cape Cod Lucky: In Another Time*. Brewster, MA: Stony Brook Publishing, 2000.

———. *Once Upon Cape Cod: From Cockle Cove to the Powder Hole*. Brewster, MA: Stony Brook Publishing, 1997.

Finch, Robert, ed. *A Place Apart: A Cape Cod Reader*. Woodstock, VT: Countryman Press, 2009.

Guild, Alice. *Growing Food and the Story of the Old Mill: The Old Windmill*. Chatham, MA: Chatham Historical Society, 1976. Brochure.

Hunt, Peter. *Peter Hunt's Cape Cod Cookbook*. New York: Gramercy Publishing Company, 1962.

Ives, Josephine. *A Beacon for Chatham: Eldredge Public Library: The First Hundred Years*. Chatham, MA: Friends of the Eldredge Public Library, 1996.

Jonas, Connie K. *That Which Brought Us Hither: The History of Harding Shores*. 2nd ed. N.p., 2005.

Lane, Ferdinand C. *On Old Cape Cod*. N.p., 1961.

Lincoln, Joseph C. *The Bradshaws of Harniss*. New York: D. Appleton-Century Company, 1943.

———. *Cape Cod Yesterdays*. New York: Blue Ribbon Books, 1935.

Monbleau, Marcia J. *Home Song Chatham*. Chatham, MA: Chatham Historical Society, 1995.

Morgan, William. *The Cape Cod Cottage*. New York: Princeton Architectural Press, 2006.

Nathan, Robert. *Journal for Josephine*. New York: Alfred A. Knopf, 1943.

Nickerson, Joshua Atkins, II. *Days to Remember: A Chatham Native Recalls Life on Cape Cod Since the Turn of the Century*. Chatham, MA: Chatham Historical Society, 1988.

O'Connell, James C. *Becoming Cape Cod: Creating a Seaside Resort*. Hanover: University of New Hampshire, 2003.

Reports of the Town Officers of the Town of Chatham. Chatham, MA: Chatham Monitor Print, published annually.

Reynard, Elizabeth. *Cahaba Verses*. N.p., 1962.

———. *The Mutinous Wind: A Sorcerer's Tale*. Cambridge, MA: Riverside Press, 1951.

———. *The Narrow Land: Folk Chronicles of Old Cape Cod*. 5th ed. Chatham, MA: Chatham Historical Society, 1978.

Snow, Edward Rowe. *A Pilgrim Returns to Cape Cod*. Boston: Yankee Publishing Co., 1946.

Taylor, Phoebe Atwood. *Punch with Care*. New York: W.W. Norton & Company, 1946.

Tougias, Michael J., and Casey Sherman. *The Finest Hours: The True Story of the U.S. Coast Guard's Most Daring Sea Rescue.* New York: Scribner, 2009.

Webber, Bernard C. *Chatham: "The Lifeboatmen."* Orleans, MA: Lower Cape Publishing Company, 1985.

Wood, Donald. *Cape Cod: A Guide.* Boston: Little, Brown, 1973.

Yacobian, John. *Cannon on Bassing Harbor: A Brief History of Cannon Hill.* N.p., 2007.

OTHER HELPFUL SOURCES

Bingham, Sallie. *Passion and Prejudice: A Family Memoir.* New York: Knopf, 1989.

Buderi, Robert. *The Invention that Changed the World.* New York: Simon & Schuster, 1996.

Budiansky, Stephen. *Battle of Wits: The Complete Story of Codebreaking in World War II.* New York: Simon & Schuster, 2000.

Delaney, William P., and William W. Ward. "Radar Development at Lincoln Laboratory: A Fifty-Year Review." *Lincoln Laboratory Journal* 12, no. 2 (2000).

D'Entremont, Jeremy. *The Lighthouse Handbook: New England.* Kennebunkport, ME: Cider Mill Press, 2008.

———. *The Lighthouses of Massachusetts.* Beverly, MA: Commonwealth Editions, 2007.

Faderman, Lillian. *To Believe in Women: What Lesbians Have Done for America—A History.* Boston: Houghton Mifflin Company, 1999.

Gildersleeve, Virginia Crocheron. *Many a Good Crusade: Memoirs.* New York: MacMillan Company, 1954.

Harrison, Gilbert A. *The Enthusiast: A Life of Thornton Wilder.* New York: Ticknor & Fields, 1983.

Hughes, Ted. *Birthday Letters.* New York: Farrar, Straus and Giroux, 1998.

Jakle, John A., Keith A. Sculle and Jefferson S. Rogers. *The Motel in America.* Baltimore: Johns Hopkins University Press, 1996.

Kraig, Bruce. *Hot Dog: A Global History.* London: Reaktion Books, 2009.

Kukil, Karen V., ed. *The Unabridged Journals of Sylvia Plath, 1950–1962.* New York: Anchor Books, 2000.

Louchheim, Mary. *My Crowd.* N.p., 2003.

McElheny, Victor K. *Insisting on the Impossible: The Life of Edwin Land.* Cambridge, MA: Perseus Books, 1998.

Oshinsky, David M. *Polio: An American Story: The Crusade that Mobilized the Nation Against the 20ᵗʰ Century's Most Feared Disease.* New York: Oxford University Press, 2005.

Plath, Aurelia Schober, ed. *Letters Home by Sylvia Plath: Correspondence 1950– 1963.* New York: Harper & Row, 1975.

Smith, Jane. S. *Patenting the Sun: Polio and the Salk Vaccine.* New York: Anchor Books, 1990.

Stallknecht, Alice. "Something of My Past." Unpublished memoir, n.d.

Swift, Will. *The Roosevelts and the Royals. Franklin and Eleanor, the King and Queen of England, and the Friendship that Changed History.* Hoboken, NJ: John Wiley & Sons, Inc., 2004.

Tifft, Susan E., and Alex S. Jones. *The Patriarch: The Rise and Fall of the Bingham Dynasty.* New York: Summit Books, 1991.

Urofsky, Melvin I. *Louis D. Brandeis: A Life.* New York: Pantheon Books, 2009.

Van Dine, Lynn C. *The Search for Peter Hunt.* Pittsburgh, PA: Local History Company, 2003.

Wilder, Robin G., and Jackson R. Bryer, eds. *The Selected Letters of Thornton Wilder.* New York: HarperCollins, 2008.

Winterbotham, F.W. *The Ultra Secret.* New York: Harper & Row, 1974.

About the Author

Debra Lawless is a freelance writer living in Chatham. She earned a BA in history and classics at Stanford University and an MS in journalism at Boston University. A native of Providence, Rhode Island, she has worked for several newspapers and as a political press secretary. Currently, she writes for the *Cape Cod Chronicle*, specializing in books and authors. She is interested in historic preservation and the visual arts. Her first book was *Chatham in the Jazz Age*.

Visit us at
www.historypress.net